THE
BIG
BOOK
OF
CHURCH
JOKES

THE BIG BOOK OF CHURCH JOKES

with cartoons by
Len Jones & Dennis Daniel

BARBOUR
PUBLISHING

ISBN 978-1-60260-386-8

Published by Barbour Publishing, Inc., P.O. Box 719, Uhrichsville, Ohio 44683
www.barbourbooks.com

*Our mission is to publish and distribute inspirational products offering
exceptional value and biblical encouragement to the masses.*

 Member of the
Evangelical Christian
Publishers Association

Printed in the United States of America.

Contents

Introduction

The eleventh commandment:
Thou shalt laugh every now and then!

Let's see: The second of the Bible's "fruits of the Spirit" is *joy*—so there must be some kind of fun in the faith life. And that's what *The Big Book of Church Jokes* is all about!

This collection of hundreds of jokes, funny stories, one-liners, and cartoons will put a smile on even the most dour church lady's face. It's all clean and good-natured humor, and arranged by topics—from pastors, deacons, and missionaries, to the people in the pews and the kids in Sunday school. You'll also find jokes on old-time church, country church, visitors, weddings, funerals—even heaven.

You'll probably see someone you know in these pages—admit it, maybe even yourself! But that's okay. If we can laugh at our own flaws, maybe we can overlook some of the foibles of others.

The Big Book of Church Jokes is ready to spread a little joy in the world. So go ahead—laugh a bit!

Pastors

Over the years of their marriage, a pastor's wife had begun signaling her husband throughout his sermons. When she discreetly touched her hand to the top of her hair, she was telling him the message was going over the people's heads. When she pulled at her ear lobe, she was asking him to speak louder. When she drew her fingers lightly across her throat, she was telling him it was time to cut the message short.

One Sunday morning, the pastor became so caught up in his message that he forgot to look his wife's way for some time. After nearly a half hour, he glanced her way—to see her holding her nose.

✛ ✛ ✛

"It's time to get up for church," a mother told her son. "You know today is Sunday."

"I don't want to go," he replied. "I don't have any friends there. The music is awful. And the sermons are boring!"

"But you have to go," the mother insisted. "You're the pastor!"

✛ ✛ ✛

Q: What do they call pastors in Germany?
A: German shepherds.

✛ ✛ ✛

"Next week I plan to preach about the sin of lying," a pastor told his congregation. "To help you understand my sermon, I would like you all to read Mark chapter 17."

The following Sunday, the preacher asked how many of his members had read the assigned chapter. Many hands went up.

"Mark has only sixteen chapters," the pastor said, smiling. "I will now proceed with my sermon on the sin of lying."

An airplane flew into a violent thunderstorm and experienced a lot of turbulence. One very nervous flier happened to be sitting next to a clergyman. "Can't you do something?" she pleaded.

"I'm sorry, ma'am," the reverend said gently. "I'm in sales, not management."

A young intern was substituting for the church's pastor, a popular minister who had suddenly become ill. The young man, though obviously nervous, presented his sermon well and then concluded his prayer with a heartfelt, "And may Pastor Hale be filled with fresh veal and new zigor!"

Some pastors' sermons are like the peace of God. They surpass all understanding.

A new preacher was delivering his first sermon and was quite nervous. He became even more concerned when he noticed that he didn't have the attention of the congregation.

"Can you hear me in the back?" he questioned.

"Not really," was the reply, whereupon everyone in the first several rows got up and moved to the back.

A man heard the airplane stewardess address his seatmate as "Doctor."

"You're a doctor, huh?" he asked. "I've been wanting to ask one of you about this pain I've been having in my side."

The doctor smiled pleasantly. "I doubt I could be of much help to you," he said. "My training is in homiletics."

"Homiletics," the man said, gasping. "Is that fatal?"

An opinionated woman attended a church service to hear a young minister. At the conclusion of the service someone asked her what she thought of his message.

"He sure spoke in true apostolic style," she commented. "He took a text and went everywhere preaching the gospel."

✦ ✦ ✦

An old man had been a faithful Christian and was in the hospital, near death. The family called their pastor to stand with them.

As the pastor stood next to the bed, the old man's condition appeared to deteriorate rapidly and he motioned frantically for something to write on. The pastor lovingly handed him a pen and a piece of paper, and the man used every ounce of strength to scribble a note before he died.

The pastor thought it best not to look at the note at that time, so he placed it in his jacket pocket.

At the funeral, as he was finishing the message, he realized that he was wearing the same jacket that he had been wearing when the man died. He said, "You know, he handed me a note just before he died. I haven't looked at it, but knowing him, I'm sure there's a word of inspiration there for us all."

He opened the note and turned pale as he read aloud the words, "You're standing on my oxygen tube!"

✦ ✦ ✦

The pastor was looking over the nativity scene the day after Christmas when he noticed that the baby Jesus was missing. He went outside and saw a little boy pulling a new red wagon. In the wagon was Jesus.

He walked up to the boy and said, "Hi, there. Where did you get the baby Jesus?"

The boy answered honestly and without remorse, "In the church."

"Why did you take him?" the pastor asked.

"Well," said the boy, "I asked Jesus for a wagon for Christmas. I told Him that if He gave me one, I'd give Him a ride in it."

✝ ✝ ✝

One Easter Sunday the minister invited all the young children to come to the front of the sanctuary for a children's sermon. The children were in their new Easter outfits and the pastor couldn't help noticing one especially pretty blond-haired, blue-eyed girl about five or six years old. She was wearing a white frilly dress, with rows and rows of ruffles head to toe—but she had a sad expression on her face.

Trying to cheer her up, the minister called her by name, and said "You look *so* lovely this morning. And I know you will wear that dress a lot because it is just beautiful."

The girl shook her head, and said, "No, Preacher, I don't think I'll ever wear this dress again."

Naturally, he couldn't imagine that response, so he said, "But you look so beautiful in that dress."

The little girl said, "Well, thank you, Preacher, but I will never wear this dress again."

The minister said, "Why do you say that?"

She rolled her eyes and said quite loudly, "Because my momma says it's such a *pain* to iron!"

One Sunday morning a small boy said to his pastor, "When I grow up I'm going to give you some money."

"Well, thank you," his pastor said. "But why?"

"Because my daddy said you're the poorest preacher we ever had."

A pastor was delivering a strong message on the evils of alcohol. Rather loudly he said, "If I had all the wine in the world, I'd dump it in the river." Even louder he declared, "If I had all the beer in the world, I'd dump it in the river." Finally he pounded the pulpit and ended his sermon by exclaiming, "If I had all the whiskey in the world, I'd dump it in the river." The music director rose for the final hymn and said with a crooked grin, "Please turn to hymn 108, 'Shall We Gather at the River?' "

✚ ✚ ✚

You might be a preacher if:

- You've been told to get a "real job."
- You've been asked, "What's so hard about preaching?"
- You've been told, "No one could pay me enough to do your job."
- Others wished they only had to work one day a week for a whole week's pay.
- You've been told that you get a week's pay for only three hours of work. You work one hour on Sunday morning, one hour on Sunday night, and one hour on Wednesday night.
- You have a fishing boat named "Visitation."
- You win a door prize at the church banquet and people complain the contest was rigged.
- You name your bed "The Word."
- You've ever said, "I'm *never* going to be a preacher!"
- You wear your new shoes to church and someone comments, "We are paying you too much money!"
- You couldn't sell used cars.
- You're awakened in the middle of the night by a couple wanting to get married so you wake your wife and daughter to be "witnesses." You all get dressed for the ceremony. When it's over the groom asks, "How much do I owe you?" You jokingly reply, "Whatever you think she's worth." After a moment the groom puts a quarter in your hand and the couple leaves.

A pastor, just out of seminary, was invited to speak at a chapel service in a prison. He was excited but this being his first time, he was nervous as well. He thought about how he would introduce his message. When he arrived at the prison, he was greeted by a large group of prisoners waiting to hear him. As the young pastor stood behind the podium, he said, "Good morning. It's so good that you're all here!"

A man lost two buttons from his shirt and put them in his pants pocket. But the pocket had a hole, so the buttons fell into his shoe. Unfortunately, the shoe sole also had a hole, so he lost the buttons. As pockets with holes, holes without buttons, and shoe soles with holes are useless, the man ripped the buttonholes out of his shirt and the pocket from his pants and tossed them in the trash along with the soles of his shoes. A police officer who was observing the man asked him for some identification. The man gave the officer a document that showed he was an ordained minister of the gospel. When the officer began to escort him to a mental institution, the minister protested violently, asking why he was receiving such unjust treatment. "Look, we both know it's the best place for you now," the officer replied. "Anyone claiming to be a preacher who doesn't save souls or wear holy clothes has probably lost his buttons."

When a brand-new pastor arrived at his first church, several of the "Great Old Saints" who had been waiting to die did just that. Consequently, in four weeks the pastor did eight funerals. Because he was so busy and exhausted, he did not have time to write his regular Sunday sermons—and so he used the sermon from the Sunday before three more times. When members of the congregation complained to the bishop, the bishop asked what the sermon was about. The members paused, scratching their heads. The bishop said, "He better use it one more time."

✚ ✚ ✚

A young pastor was sitting in a restaurant eating lunch. He opened a letter he'd just received that morning from his mom. As he opened it a twenty-dollar bill fell out. He thought to himself, *Thanks, Mom, I sure needed that right now.* As he finished his meal he noticed a beggar outside on the sidewalk leaning against the light post. Thinking that the poor man could probably use the twenty dollars more than he, he crossed out the names on the envelope and wrote across the top in large letters, Persevere! So as not to make a scene, he put the envelope under his arm and dropped it as he walked past the man. The man picked it up and read the message and smiled. The next day, as the pastor enjoyed his meal, the same man tapped him on the shoulder and handed him a big wad of bills. Surprised, the young pastor asked him what that was for. The man replied, "This is your half of the winnings. Persevere came in first in the fourth race at the track yesterday and paid thirty to one."

One preacher said, "My sermons are like chickens with their heads cut off. Once you think the sermon is done, it just jumps back up and runs in another direction!"

A rule of thumb for preachers: If after ten minutes you haven't struck oil, stop boring!

One Sunday a pastor announced to his congregation, "It's a beautiful day to worship. My good people, I have here in my hands three sermons. . .a $1000 sermon that lasts five minutes, a $500 sermon that lasts fifteen minutes, and a $100 sermon that lasts a full hour. We'll take the collection and see which one I'll deliver."

✠ ✠ ✠

A preacher stepped to the pulpit with an adhesive bandage on his chin. "I'm sorry about this," he said self-consciously. "I cut my chin this morning when I was thinking about my sermon." Someone from the congregation replied, "Next time why not think about your chin and cut the sermon?"

✝ ✝ ✝

At a preacher's convention a pastor got up and started his sermon with this sentence: "I spent the best years of my life in the arms of a woman not my wife." As the congregation gasped he quickly said, "She was my mother!" The congregation chuckled and a young preacher tucked it into his memory to use with his own congregation. Back home he began to feel a bit uncertain that he remembered it right. Forging ahead anyway, he started with, "I spent the best years of my life in the arms of a woman not my wife." The congregation gasped and the preacher paused, forgetting the punch line. After a few nervous moments he stammered, "And I can't remember who she was!"

A seminary student was preaching his first sermon. He meant to say, "God called me to heal the sick, raise the dead, and cast out the devil." However, he was quite nervous and what he actually said was, "God called me to heal the dead, cast out the sick, and raise the devil."

A new seminary graduate, wanting to show off his intelligence, said to the older preacher, "In order to effectively instruct the masses, it is incumbent upon us that we, in a most articulate fashion, rightly disseminate the word of truth. In order to avoid the presence of psychological processing and theoretical reasoning, which only capitulates to philosophical conclusiveness and diminishes one's assiduous approach to the charismatic overview of the divine holy writ, which in the end, ultimately leads to spiritual interposition and characteristic nullification in the Christian life. . . ." The older preacher replied, "In other words, if we don't go to Bible study, we'll be too smart to know how dumb we really are."

Why can't preachers get to sleep at night? They count lost sheep.

When the flight attendant asked the pastor why he was nervous, he replied, "The Bible says '*Lo*, I am with you always.' "

A young girl's parents decided to take her to visit a new church one Sunday morning. As a small bribe, they told her that if she were good during the service they would take her to her favorite restaurant afterward.

During the pastor's rather fiery sermon on the destination of the good versus the destination of the evil he asked, in a rather loud voice, "And where do you think those who live a pure, just, and good life before the Lord are going to go?"

The girl stood in her seat and cried out, "To my favorite restaurant!"

After church one Sunday morning, a young boy suddenly announced to his mother, "Mom, I think I'll be a minister when I grow up."

"That's great, but what made you decide that?"

"Well," said the little boy, "I have to go to church on Sunday anyway, and I figure it will be more fun to stand up and yell than to sit and listen."

When a pastor became ill one Sunday morning, he called on a retired pastor in the congregation to fill in for him. The substitute agreed, but with some reservations since the regular pastor was well loved by the people. When the old preacher entered the pulpit, he grasped for an illustration that would convey his humility in the task.

"I feel inadequate in taking the place of your minister this morning. He is such a good preacher and brings light just like sunlight through a clean pane of glass. I, on the other hand, am like the piece of cardboard that has been substituted for the pane in the window."

He went on to preach a decent sermon. At the door afterward a well-meaning lady grasped his hand. "Preacher, you're no cardboard. You're a real pane."

The minister was waiting up for his teenaged daughter who was out far past her curfew. When she finally came home around 3:00 a.m. he bellowed, "Good morning, child of the devil!"

The girl answered respectfully, "Good morning, Father."

A pastor was riding his horse down the road one day when one of the members of the congregation spotted him. "Preacher, do you realize your horse looks better than you do?" the person said.

"Yes, I know," he said. "I take care of my horse. My congregation takes care of me."

A preacher died. Shortly thereafter a man with the same name went on a business trip to a southern state. He sent a telegram to his wife, but it was delivered to the preacher's wife by mistake. It said, "Arrived safely. Sure is hot here!"

A pastor went out one Saturday to visit his church members. At one house, though it was obvious that someone was home, nobody came to the door, even after the preacher knocked several times. Finally, the preacher took out his card and wrote "Revelation 3:20" on the back of it and stuck it in the door. (The verse says: "Behold, I stand at the door and knock. If anyone hears my voice and opens the door, I will come in to him and dine with him, and he with me.") At the next service the card turned up in the collection plate. Below the preacher's message the church member left a message of his own: "I heard your voice in the garden, and I was afraid because I was naked; and I hid myself"—Genesis 3:10.

A pastor, known for his lengthy sermons, noticed a man get up and leave during the middle of his message, only to return just before the conclusion of the service. The pastor was curious about where the man had been, so he asked him.

"I went to get a haircut," was the reply.

"Why didn't you do that before the service?" the pastor asked.

"Because," the gentleman said, "I didn't need one then."

A pastor was walking down the street one day when he noticed a small boy across the street struggling to ring a doorbell.

After watching the boy's efforts for some time, the pastor walked across the street and placed his hand kindly on the child's shoulder before leaning over to give the doorbell a solid ring.

Crouching down to the child's level, the pastor smiled benevolently and asked, "And now what, my little man?" To which the boy replied, "Now we run!"

+ + +

A minister's widow, who was a little old-fashioned, was planning a week's vacation in a national park. Before she went, though, she decided to write a letter addressing the state of the accommodations, particularly the bathroom facilities. Because she was too delicate to write the word *toilet* in a letter, she settled on "bathroom commode." But when she wrote that down, it still sounded too crude so, after the first page of her letter, she referred to the facilities simply as *BC*. She wrote: "Does the cabin where I will be staying have its own *BC*? If not, where is the *BC* located?"

The campground owner took the first page of the letter with the woman's check and gave it to his secretary. He put the second page of the letter on the desk of the senior member of his staff without noticing that the staffer would have no way of knowing what *BC* meant. Then the owner went off to town to run some errands.

The staff member came in after lunch and found the letter—and then answered the woman's queries to the best of his ability. When he discovered the woman was the widow of a famous Baptist preacher, he was sure that *BC* stood for "Baptist Church."

Dear Madam,
I regret very much the delay in answering your letter, but I now take the pleasure in informing you that the *BC* is located nine miles north of the campground and is capable of seating 250 people at one time. I admit it is quite a distance away if you are in the habit of going regularly, but no doubt you will be pleased to know that a great number of people take their lunches along and make a day of it. They usually arrive early and stay late.

The last time my wife and I went was six years ago, and it was so crowded we had to stand up the whole time we were there. It may interest you to know that right now there is a supper planned to raise money to buy more seats. They are going to hold it in the basement of the *BC*.

I would like to say that it pains me very much not to be able to go more regularly, but it is surely no lack of desire on my part. As we grow older, it seems to be more of an effort, particularly in cold weather.

If you decide to come down to our campground, perhaps I could go with you the first time, sit with you, and introduce you to all the folks. Remember, this is a friendly community.

Comedian George Burns is said to have noted, "The secret of a good sermon is to have a good beginning and a good ending; and to have the two as close together as possible."

The new minister stood at the church door greeting the members as they left the Sunday morning service. While most of the people told the minister how much they liked his message, one man seemingly had a different opinion. "That was a very dull and boring sermon, Pastor," he said. The pastor was a bit baffled by this, but he continued shaking hands.

A few minutes later, the same man again appeared in line and said, "I don't think you did much in the way of preparation for your message."

Once again, the man circled back and appeared in line, this time muttering, "You really blew it. You didn't have a thing to say, Pastor."

Finally, the minister could stand it no longer. He went to one of the deacons and inquired about the man." Oh, don't let that guy bother you," said the deacon. "He's a little slow. All he does is go around repeating whatever he hears other people saying."

A minister delivered a sermon in ten minutes one Sunday morning, which was about half the usual length of his sermons. He explained, "I am sorry to inform you that my dog, who is fond of eating paper, ate the last portion of my sermon and I have nothing more to say." After the service, a visitor from another church shook hands with the preacher and said, "Pastor, if that dog of yours has any pups, I'd like to get one for my pastor."

Two women were talking about their pastors.

One woman: "My pastor is so good he can talk on any subject for an hour."

The other: "That's pretty good, but my pastor has him beat. He can talk for an hour without a subject!"

A preacher phoned the city's newspaper. "Thank you very much for the error you made when you printed my sermon topic for last Sunday. The topic I sent you was 'What Jesus Saw in a Publican.' What really appeared was 'What Jesus Saw in a Republican.' I had the biggest crowd of the year!"

The chairman of the pastoral search committee informed the congregation, "Next Sunday our visiting preacher will be the Reverend Jones. If you wish to see the other preacher candidates, you will find them hanging in the vestibule."

Nineteenth-century Baptist preacher Charles H. Spurgeon once said, "Some ministers would make good martyrs; they are so dry they would burn well."

✦ ✦ ✦

A pastor was tired of hearing excuses why people fail to attend church, so he included this list in the Sunday bulletin.

TEN REASONS WHY I NEVER WASH:
I was forced to as a child.
People who wash are hypocrites—they think they're cleaner than everybody else.
There are so many different kinds of soap, how would I decide which is best.
I used to wash, but I got bored and stopped.
I wash only on special occasions, like Christmas and Easter.
None of my friends washes.
I'll start washing when I get older and dirtier.
I can't spare the time.
The bathroom is never warm enough in winter or cool enough in summer.
People who make soap are only after your money.

"I DON'T KNOW WHY THAT SERMON BOMBED. IT WAS ONE OF BILLY GRAHAM'S BEST."

A minister was opening his mail one morning. One envelope contained a single sheet of paper on which was written only one word: FOOL.

The next Sunday he announced, "I have known many people who have written letters and forgotten to sign their name. But this week I received a letter from someone who signed his name but has forgotten to write a letter."

A minister was pulled over for speeding. As the cop was about to write the ticket, the minister said to him, "Blessed are the merciful, for they shall obtain mercy."

The cop handed the minister the ticket and said, "Go thou and sin no more."

A pastor parked in a no-parking zone in a large city because he was in a hurry and couldn't find a space with a meter. Concerned, he put a note under the wiper that read: "I have circled the block ten times. If I don't park here, I'll miss my appointment. Forgive me my trespasses."

When he returned, he found a citation from a police officer along with this note: "I've circled this block for ten years. If I don't give you a ticket, I'll lose my job. Lead me not into temptation."

The richest man in town met with a minister after the Sunday service.

"Why does everyone call me cheap and stingy?" complained the man. "I've told everyone I'm leaving half my money to the church when I die."

The minister nodded. "It reminds me of the story about the pig and the cow. The cow was much loved by the farmer and his neighbors, while the pig was not popular at all. The pig could not understand this and asked the cow about it. 'How come you are so well liked, cow? People say you're good because you give milk and butter and cream every day. But I give more than that. From me they get bacon and ham, pork chops and more; they even pickle my feet. But no one likes me, and they love you. Why do you think that is?'

"The cow looked down at the pig and answered, 'Perhaps it's because I give while I'm still alive.' "

A minister was asked by a politician, "Name something the government can do to help the church." The minister replied, "Quit making one-dollar bills."

Three preachers sat discussing the best positions for prayer while a telephone repairperson worked nearby. "Kneeling is definitely best," claimed one.

"No," another contended. "I concentrate better while standing with my hands outstretched to heaven."

"You're both wrong," the third insisted. "The most effective prayer position is lying humbly, facedown on the floor."

The repairperson could contain himself no longer. "Hey, fellas," he interrupted. "The best prayin' I ever did was hangin' upside down from a telephone pole."

By the time the morning service was to begin, only one man was in the church.

The pastor said to him, "It looks like everyone has slept in. Do you want to go home or should I go ahead with the sermon?"

The man replied, "When I go to feed the chickens and only one comes, I still feed it."

The minister took that as a yes, mounted the pulpit, and delivered an hour-long sermon. At the end, he asked the man what he thought.

His answer: "Well, when I go to feed the chickens and only one comes, I don't give her the entire bucket!"

✠ ✠ ✠

At the conclusion of the sermon, the worshippers filed out of the sanctuary to greet the minister. As one shook the minister's hand, he said, "Thanks for the message, Reverend. You know, I bet you're smarter than Einstein."

Beaming with pride, the minister said, "Why, thank you, brother!"

As the week went by, the minister began to think about the man's compliment. The more he thought, the more he wondered why anyone would deem him smarter than Einstein. So the following Sunday he asked the man, "Exactly what did you mean that I must be smarter than Einstein?"

The man replied, "Well, Reverend, they say that Einstein was so smart that only ten people in the entire world could understand him. But Reverend, no one can understand you."

✚ ✚ ✚

A district minister arrived one Sunday morning in a small rural town. The local minister asked the district minister to help with a local problem.

"Everyone here thinks they are just perfect!" said the local minister. "Could you preach a sermon that will bring them back to their senses?"

The district minister was a gifted speaker, eloquent with words and knowledgeable about the scripture. He spoke for nearly an hour, convincing everyone that they too were sinners. Finally, the district minister was sure he had set everyone straight. To be certain that they were all thinking alike, the district minister finally asked, "Is there anyone here who thinks they are perfect?"

Everyone was looking at the floor, thinking quietly. Slowly, one man in the back stood up.

"And why do you feel you are perfect, sir?" the minister asked.

The man said, "I am not perfect, but I am standing in memory of my wife's first husband who was."

One pastor's vote for the best prayer: "Lord, please make me the kind of person my dog thinks I am."

✚ ✚ ✚

For the Preacher: Good News and Bad News

Good News: You baptized seven people today in the river.
Bad News: Two of them were taken in the current.

Good News: The Women's Guild voted to send you a get-well card.
Bad News: The vote passed by thirty to twenty-nine.

Good News: The elder board accepted your job description the way you wrote it.
Bad News: They were so inspired, they formed a search committee to find somebody who could fill the position.

Good News: You finally found a choir director who approaches things exactly the way you do.
Bad News: The choir rebelled.

Good News: Mrs. Smith is wild about your sermons.
Bad News: Mrs. Smith is also wild about celebrity tabloids and gruesome horror movies.

Good News: Your women's softball team finally won a game.
Bad News: They beat your men's softball team.

Good News: The trustees finally voted to add more church parking.
Bad News: They're going to pave the front lawn of the parsonage.

Good News: Church attendance rose dramatically the last three weeks.
Bad News: You were on vacation.

Good News: Your deacons want to send you to the Holy Land.
Bad News: They are waiting until the next war.

Good News: The youth in your church have come to your home to pay a surprise visit.
Bad News: It's midnight and they are armed with toilet paper and shaving cream.

A new preacher wanted to rent a house in the country but the only one available was rumored to be haunted. That didn't bother the preacher since he didn't believe in such things. He went ahead and rented the place.

Soon the ghost made its appearance. The preacher told his friends about the ghost, but they didn't believe him. They told him the only way they would believe was if he took a picture of the ghost.

The preacher went home and called for the ghost. When it appeared, the preacher explained the situation and asked the ghost if it would mind having its picture taken. The ghost agreed.

When the picture was developed, the ghost wasn't visible. Feeling very disappointed, the preacher called again for the ghost. When it appeared, the preacher showed it the picture and wanted to know why the ghost wasn't in it. The ghost thought a minute and replied, "Well, I guess the spirit was willing, but the flash was weak."

The pastor shocked the congregation when he announced that he was resigning from the church and moving to a warmer climate.

After the service, a very distraught lady came to the pastor with tears in her eyes. "Oh, Pastor, we are going to miss you so much. Please don't leave!"

The pastor patted her hand and said, "Now, now, don't cry. I'm sure the pastor who takes my place will be even better than me."

"Yeah," she said, with a tone of disappointment in her voice, "that's what they said the last time, too."

✦ ✦ ✦

An eighty-five-year-old matriarch hadn't been to church lately, so her minister thought he'd go pay her a visit. He knocked on her door and after a time he heard her spirited voice holler, "Hello, who is it?"

"It's Reverend ___," he answered.

"Oh, come in, come in," she said. "How's the church doing?"

"Everything is wonderful. But I just wanted to see how you are doing. We've missed you."

"Well, I haven't been feeling too well lately. I had quite the root canal last week."

Just then the phone rang and she excused herself to get it. The minister sat near a table with an old magazine and a bowl of peanuts. After a few minutes, he started flipping through the magazine. After another ten minutes or so, he heard his stomach growl and began to get restless, so he started in on the bowl of peanuts while he read. After a while, he suddenly realized that he had eaten the entire bowl of peanuts.

Just then the woman returned and said, "I sure do apologize. That was my sister from Baltimore. She only calls once per month so when she does we have to catch up on everything."

The minister, feeling a little embarrassed, said, "I must also apologize. While you were gone I got hungry and ate all the peanuts in your little bowl there."

The woman began to chuckle. "Oh that's okay, Pastor. Since the root canal, the best I can do is suck all the chocolate off of 'em!"

✛ ✛ ✛

The preacher's topic for his sermon was "Forgive Your Enemies." At the end he asked how many were willing to forgive their enemies. About half the congregation held up their hands. Not satisfied, he continued on for another twenty minutes and repeated his question. This time he had a better response, but it still wasn't 100 percent. So he continued for another fifteen minutes and repeated his question. With all thoughts now on Sunday dinner, everyone responded except one elderly woman in the rear of the church. "Are you not willing to forgive your enemies?" the pastor asked.

"I don't have any."

"That is very unusual. How old are you?"

"Ninety-three."

"Please come down in front and tell the congregation how a person can live to ninety-three and not have an enemy in the world."

The woman teetered down the aisle and very slowly turned around. "It's easy. I just outlived them all!"

✛ ✛ ✛

If the church wants a better preacher, it only needs to pray for the one it has.

✛ ✛ ✛

Top Ten Signs You Are in for a Long Sermon

10. There's a cooler of bottled water beside the pulpit.
9. The pews have camper hookups.
8. You overhear the pastor telling the sound man to

have a few dozen extra tapes on hand to record today's sermon.

7. The preacher has brought a snack to the pulpit.

6. The preacher breaks for an intermission.

5. The bulletins have pizza delivery and take-out menus.

4. When the preacher asks the deacon to bring in his notes, he rolls in a filing cabinet.

3. The choir loft has recliners instead of pews.

2. Instead of taking off his watch and laying it on the pulpit, the preacher turns over a four-foot hourglass.

And the number-one sign you are in for a long sermon:

1. The minister says, "You'll be out in time to watch the Super Bowl"—but it's only September!

The seminary's dean of admissions was interviewing a prospective student. "Why have you chosen this career?" he asked.

"I dream of making a million dollars in the pastorate, like my father," the student replied.

"Your father made a million dollars in the pastorate?" echoed the dean, quite shocked.

"No," replied the applicant. "But he always dreamed of it."

A minister was on top of a hill one day when a flood swept through the town. As the water was rising rapidly, the Coast Guard was dispatched and came to the pastor's aid. "Reverend, come aboard so you don't drown!"

The minister replied, "No thanks, the Lord will save me."

The water climbed even higher and the Coast Guard came back again. But still the minister replied, "The Lord will save me."

The Coast Guard came one more time but with no luck in getting the minister on the boat. The water finally reached the top of the hill and the minister drowned.

In heaven, the minister asked God, "Father, why didn't You save me?"

God replied, "Well, I sent the Coast Guard to pick you up three times!"

A doctor, a professor, a preacher, and a young boy were taking a ride in a small private plane. Suddenly the engine began to sputter. In spite of the pilot's best efforts, the plane started to go down. In terror, the pilot grabbed a parachute and bailed out. Unfortunately there were only three chutes remaining.

The doctor said, "I'm a physician—I save lives, so I must save myself." He grabbed a parachute and jumped. The professor then said, "I'm one of the most intelligent people in our whole country. I have to teach the next generation, so I'm taking a parachute." He grabbed a pack and jumped, too.

The preacher embraced the little boy and said, "Son, I've enjoyed a long and full life. You're young and have your whole life ahead of you. Take the last parachute and go!"

The boy handed the parachute back to the preacher and said, "Not to worry, Reverend. The smartest man in the world just jumped out of the plane with my backpack."

A minister was asked to dinner by a parishioner he knew to be an unkempt housekeeper. When he sat down at the table, he noticed that the dishes were filthier than any he'd seen in his life. "Were these dishes ever washed?" he asked his hostess, running his fingers over the grit and grime.

She replied, "Sure, they're as clean as soap and water could get them."

He felt a bit apprehensive but blessed the food anyway and started eating. It was really delicious and he said so, despite the disgusting dishes. When dinner was over, the hostess took the dishes outside and yelled to her two dogs, "Here, Soap! Here, Water!"

✣ ✣ ✣

A group of Methodist ministers was attending an annual conference at a private countryside resort. As several set off to explore the area, they came upon an old bridge that crossed a quiet pond.

Unfortunately, they didn't notice a sign warning of the bridge's unsafe condition. As they crossed it, the caretaker came running after them. "Hey! Get off that bridge!" he yelled.

"It's all right," declared one of the ministers. "We're all Methodist ministers attending the conference."

"That's fine," replied the caretaker. "But if you don't get off that bridge, you'll all be Baptists!"

The young couple invited their aged pastor for Sunday dinner. While they were in the kitchen preparing the meal, the minister asked their son what they were having. "Goat," the little boy replied. Finding this a bit unusual, the pastor said, "Goat? Are you sure about that?"

"Sure," said the child confidently. "I heard Pa say to Ma, 'Might as well have the old goat for dinner today as any other day.' "

A tired pastor was at home resting when he looked through the window and saw a woman approaching his door. She was one of those talkative people and he wasn't in the mood to deal with her. He said to his wife, "I'll just duck upstairs and wait until she goes away."

An hour passed, then he tiptoed to the stair landing and listened. . .not a sound. As he started down the stairs, he called loudly to his wife, "Well, my dear, did you get rid of that old bore at last?"

The next moment he heard the voice of the obnoxious woman caller, and she couldn't possibly have missed hearing him. Two steps down, he saw them both staring up at him. It seemed truly a crisis moment. But his wife came to the rescue. "Yes, dear, she went away over an hour ago. But Mrs. Anderson has come to call in the meantime, and I'm sure you'll be glad to greet her."

The substitute Sunday school teacher was having trouble with the combination lock on the supply cabinet. She had been told the combination but it just didn't seem to be working. Finally she went to the pastor's study and asked for help. The pastor came into the room and began to turn the dial. After the first two numbers he paused and stared blankly for a moment. Finally he looked serenely heavenward and his lips moved silently. Then he looked back at the lock and quickly turned to the final number and opened the lock. The teacher was amazed. "Your faith amazes me, Pastor," she said. "It's really nothing," he answered. "The number is taped to the ceiling."

A pastor allowed time for prayer requests at the beginning of each service. When someone requested prayer for an upcoming biopsy, the pastor had a mental lapse. Instead, he asked everyone to pray for the person's autopsy.

One Sunday afternoon, the pastor's wife dropped into an easy chair saying, "Boy, am I ever exhausted! I really need a nap."

Her husband looked over at her and said, "I had to deliver two special messages last night and three today, a total of five sermons. Why are *you* so tired?"

"Dearest," she replied, "I had to listen to all of them."

When a bishop visited a church in his diocese, only three people arrived for the service. He asked the vicar, "Did you let them know I would be coming?"

"No," replied the vicar, "but word seems to have gotten around anyway."

At Christmas the pastor received a fruitcake from a well-meaning woman in the church. However, the fruitcake was so dry and flavorless that the pastor's family just couldn't swallow it. They regretfully threw it out.

Wanting to be kind and yet truthful when thanking the woman, the pastor said, "We appreciate your gift, and let me assure you that a fruitcake like that never lasts long in our home."

During a sermon, two teenaged girls were giggling and disturbing others. The pastor stopped his message to announce, "Someone here is not getting much out of this message." The girls took the hint and quieted down.

After the service, the pastor was greeting church members at the sanctuary door. Three adults apologized for sleeping in church and promised never to do so again.

At the one-hundredth anniversary of a church, several former pastors and the bishop were in attendance. At one point, our minister had the children gather at the altar for a talk about the importance of the day. He began by asking them, "Does anyone know what the bishop does?"

After a minute of silence, one brave little boy answered gravely, "He's the one you can move diagonally."

During a Sunday service, the pastor gave his parishioners an opportunity for prayer requests. There were the usual requests to pray for the sick, missionaries, servicemen and women, and so on. The somber mood was broken when the last request was made. A woman stood up and said, "My granddaughter turned sixteen this week and received her driver's license. Let us pray for us all."

During an ice storm a pastor went to check the mailbox, carefully shuffling down the driveway. When he reached for the mail, his feet went straight up in the air and he landed on his back. More embarrassed than hurt, he looked to see if anyone witnessed his fall and spied an ambulance passing by.

When the paramedics climbed out of the truck to assist him, one said, "It's the preacher!" Then he turned to the pastor and said, "Are you okay?"

"I just got the wind knocked out of me," he replied.

"Wow," said another medic. "It takes a lot to knock the wind out of a preacher!"

✛ ✛ ✛

One Sunday, a guest minister noticed in the bulletin an order of worship with which he was unfamiliar. Since the service had already begun, he was unable to ask anybody about it. So when that particular part of the service arrived, he swallowed his pride and asked from the pulpit, "What do I do now?" Someone in the congregation shouted back, "You say something and we respond."

Embarrassed, he admitted, "For the first time in my life, I'm speechless."

And the congregation responded, "Thanks be to God."

✛ ✛ ✛

"Every member of this church is going to die someday."

Then the pastor noticed that a man in the congregation began to grin. Thinking the man hadn't heard him, the pastor repeated the same sentence several times, in a louder voice each time. The man was almost laughing by now.

Perplexed, at the end of the service the pastor cornered the man and asked him why he was so happy.

The man replied, "I'm not a member of this church."

✚ ✚ ✚

The Perfect Pastor

—The Perfect Pastor preaches exactly ten minutes. He condemns sin roundly, but never hurts anyone's feelings. He works from 8:00 a.m. until midnight, and also cleans the church.
—The Perfect Pastor makes forty dollars a week, wears name-brand clothes, drives a good car, buys good books, and donates thirty dollars a week to the parish. He is twenty-nine years old and has forty years' worth of experience. Above all, he is quite attractive.
—The Perfect Pastor has a burning desire to work with young people, and he spends most of his time volunteering in the local senior center. He smiles all the time with a straight face because he has a sense of humor that keeps him seriously dedicated to his parish. He makes fifteen home visits a day but is always in his office when needed.
—The Perfect Pastor always has time for the parish and all of the church committees. He never misses the meeting of any parish organization and is always busy evangelizing the unchurched. He never fails to attend every church and worthwhile community function.
—The Perfect Pastor is always in the next parish over!

The visiting preacher was really getting the congregation moving. Near the end of his sermon he said, "This church has really got to walk," to which someone in the back yelled, "Let her walk, Preacher!" The preacher then said, "If this church is going to move, it's got to get up and run"—to which someone again yelled with enthusiasm, "Let her run, Preacher!" Feeling the excitement of the moment, the preacher then said even louder, "If this church is going to go, it's got to really fly!" Once again, with ever greater fervency, someone yelled, "Let her fly, Preacher, let her fly!" The preacher then stated with even greater gusto, "If this church is really going to fly, it's going to need money," to which someone in the back yelled, "Let her walk, Preacher, let her walk."

A preacher who had suffered extremely strained relations with his congregation was finally appointed chaplain at the state prison. Elated to be rid of him, the people came in great numbers to hear his farewell discourse. Knowing that there would be a large crowd, he carefully chose as his text, "I go and prepare a place for you. . .that where I am, there ye may be also" (John 14:3).

A boy was watching his father, a pastor, write a sermon.
   "How do you know what to say?" he asked.
   "Why, God tells me."
   "How come you hafta keep crossing things out then?"

A pastor placed his order at the pet store: "I need at least fifty mice, two thousand ants, and as many of

"I KNOW WE ARE IN FOR A HUMDINGER OF A SER-
MON. BROTHER BLOOPER TOLD ME HE STAYED UP
ALL NIGHT WORKING ON IT!"

those little silverfish as you have." The clerk replied, "We can probably do that, but it's a strange request. Mind if I ask why?" The pastor replied, "I've accepted a call to another church and the deacons told me to leave the parsonage the way I found it."

An old preacher was dying. In his last moments he sent a message for his doctor and his lawyer, both church members, to come to his home. As they entered the room the preacher held out his hands and motioned for them to sit, one on each side of his bed. The preacher grasped their hands, sighed contentedly, and smiled and stared at the ceiling.

For a time, no one said anything. Both the doctor and lawyer were flattered that the preacher would ask them to be with him during his final moments. Actually they were wondering why he would call for them as he had never particularly liked either of them. They both remembered his many long, uncomfortable sermons about greed, covetousness, and avaricious behavior that made them squirm in their seats.

Finally, the doctor said, "Preacher, why did you ask us to come?" The old preacher mustered up his strength, and then said weakly, "Jesus died between two thieves; and that's the way I want to go, too."

Three friends decided to go hunting together. One was a lawyer, one a doctor, and the other a preacher. As they were walking, along came a big buck. The three of them shot at the same time and the buck dropped immediately. The hunting party rushed to see how big it actually was. Upon reaching the fallen deer, they found out that it was dead but had only one bullet hole.

A debate followed concerning whose buck it was. When a game warden came by, he offered to help. A few moments later, he had the answer.

He said with much confidence, "The pastor shot the buck!" The friends were amazed that he could determine that so quickly and with so little examination. The game warden just smiled. "It was easy to figure out. The bullet went in one ear and out the other."

A minister was walking down the street when he came upon a group of about a dozen boys, all between ten and twelve years of age.

The group had surrounded a dog. Concerned lest the boys were hurting the dog, he went over and asked, "What are you doing with that dog?"

One of the boys replied, "This dog is just an old neighborhood stray. We all want him, but only one of us can take him home. So we've decided that whichever one of us can tell the biggest lie will get to keep the dog."

The reverend was taken aback. "What kind of contest is that?" he exclaimed. "You shouldn't be lying about anything." He then launched into a ten-minute sermon against lying, beginning with "Don't you boys know it's a sin to lie" and ending with "Why, when I was your age, I never told a lie."

There was dead silence for about a minute. Just as the reverend was beginning to think he'd gotten through to them, the smallest boy gave a deep sigh and said, "I guess we'd better give him the dog."

A pastor woke up Sunday morning and, realizing it was an exceptionally beautiful and sunny early spring day, decided the golf course was calling him. So he told the associate pastor that he was feeling sick and convinced him to deliver the sermon for him. As soon as the associate pastor left, the senior pastor headed out of town to a golf course about forty miles away where he was confident he wouldn't meet anyone he knew from his parish.

Setting up on the first tee, he was alone. After all, it was Sunday morning and everyone else was in church! At about this time, Saint Peter leaned over to the Lord while looking down from the heavens and exclaimed, "You're not going to let him get away with this, are You?" The Lord sighed, and said, "No, I won't."

Just then the pastor hit the ball and it shot straight toward the pin, dropping just short. Then the ball rolled up and fell into the hole, a 420-yard hole-in-one! Saint Peter was astonished.

He looked at the Lord and asked, "What was that all about? I thought You said You wouldn't let him get away with this!"

The Lord smiled and replied, "Who's he going to tell?"

The preacher and the choir director were not getting along and their rift was beginning to affect the worship service.

One week the preacher preached on commitment, and how we should dedicate ourselves to service. The choir director then led the song, "I Shall Not Be Moved."

The next Sunday, the preacher preached on giving and how we should gladly give tithes and offerings to the work of the Lord. The choir director then led the song, "Jesus Paid It All."

The next Sunday, the preacher preached on gossiping and how sinful it is. The choir director then led the song, "I Love to Tell the Story."

Disgusted, the preacher told the congregation the next Sunday that he was considering resigning. The choir director then led the song, "Oh, Why Not Tonight."

A few weeks later when the preacher did resign, he

told the church that Jesus had led him there and Jesus was taking him away. The choir director then led the song, "What a Friend We Have in Jesus."

A nearsighted minister glanced at the note that a woman had passed to an usher. The note read: "Her husband having gone to sea, his wife desires the prayers of the congregation for his safety." Failing to observe the punctuation, he startled his audience by announcing, "Her husband, having gone to see his wife, desires the prayers of the congregation for his safety."

Anxious about delivering his first sermon, the new preacher had gotten little sleep the week before he was to address his church. By Sunday morning, he was both exhausted and extremely nervous. Nevertheless, he managed to make it up the few steps onto the platform. He had barely begun his presentation, though, when everything he had planned to say flew right out of his mind. In fact, his mind went totally blank. Then he remembered that in seminary they had taught him what to do if a situation as this ever arose: "Repeat your last point, and let it remind you of what's coming next."

Figuring this advice couldn't hurt, he recalled the last thing he'd said and repeated it: "Behold," he quoted, "I come quickly." Still his mind was blank. He thought he'd better try it again: "Behold, I come quickly." Still nothing. He tried it one more time, but in his panic he pronounced the words with such force that he lost his balance, fell forward, knocked the pulpit to one side, tripped over a flower arrangement, and fell into the lap of a little old woman in the front row.

Flustered and embarrassed, he picked himself up, apologized profusely, and started to explain what had just happened. "Oh, that's all right, Preacher," said the woman kindly. "It was my fault, really. You told me three times you were coming quickly. I should have gotten out of your way!"

+ + +

Letters to Pastors

Dear Pastor,
Please say in your sermon that I have been a good boy all week.
I am Michael.

Dear Pastor,
I'm sorry I can't leave more money in the plate, but my father didn't give me a raise in my allowance. Could you have a sermon about a raise in my allowance?

Dear Pastor,
My mother is religious. She plays bingo at church every week even if she's sick.

Dear Pastor,
I would like to go to heaven someday because I know my brother won't be there.

Dear Pastor,
I liked your sermon where you said that good health is more important than money but I still want

a raise in my allowance.

Dear Pastor,
   Please pray for all the airline pilots. I am flying to California tomorrow.

Dear Pastor,
   I hope to go to heaven someday but later than sooner.

Dear Pastor,
   My father says I should learn the Ten Commandments. But don't you think we have enough rules already in my house?

Dear Pastor,
   Are there any devils on earth? I think there may be one in my class.

Dear Pastor,
   How does God know the good people from the bad people? Do you tell Him or does He read about it in the newspaper?

✛ ✛ ✛

A pastor was delivering a message on the evils of television. "It steals away precious time that could be used on activities of more value," he said, admonishing the congregation to do as his family had done. "We've put our television in a closet," he admitted.
   "Yes," said his disgruntled wife, "it sure gets crowded in there."

After the revival had concluded, the three pastors were discussing the results with one another.

The Methodist minister said, "The revival was wonderful for us! We gained four new families."

The Baptist preacher said, "We did well, too. We gained six new families."

The Presbyterian pastor said, "Well, we did even better than that! We got rid of our ten biggest trouble-makers!"

The preacher, who was wired for sound with a lapel microphone, moved briskly about the platform, jerking the cord as he went. Then he moved to one side, and nearly tripped over the cord. After several circles and jerks, a little girl in the third pew leaned toward her mother and whispered, "If he gets loose, will he bite?"

✠✠✠

The pastor of a church is in a precarious position—he can't please everyone. It has been said:
* If he is young, he lacks experience; if his hair is gray, he's too old to reach the young people.
* If he has several children, he has too many; if he has no children, he can't relate.
* If he preaches from his notes, he has canned sermons and is too dry; if he doesn't use notes, he has not studied and is unprepared.

* If he is attentive to the poor people in the church, they claim he is playing to the grandstand; if he pays attention to the wealthy, he is trying to be an aristocrat.
* If he suggests changes for improvement of the church, he is a dictator; if he makes no suggestions, he is weak.
* If he uses too many illustrations, he neglects the Bible; if he doesn't use enough illustrations, he is confusing.
* If he condemns wrongs, he is cranky; if he doesn't preach against sin, he's a compromiser.
* If he fails to please somebody, he's hurting the church and ought to leave; if he tries to please everyone, he is a fool.
* If he preaches about money, he's a money grabber; if he doesn't preach spiritual giving, he is failing to develop the people.
* If he drives an old car, he is an embarrassment to his congregation; if he drives a new car, he spends money unwisely.
* If he preaches all the time, the people get tired of hearing one man; if he invites guest speakers, he is shirking his responsibility.
* If he receives a large salary, he's mercenary; if he receives only a small salary, it proves he isn't worth much anyway.

✛ ✛ ✛

How do you make a small fortune as a preacher?
    Start with a large fortune.

Two brothers had felt called to go into the ministry, but they ended up in seminaries of different denominations. On their way to a family dinner, they were discussing which one of them would be asked to pray for the meal.

"After all, we both serve God," said the one brother.

"Yes, we do," replied the other, "you in your way, and I in His!"

One day each week, the pastor set aside time to visit the parish school. During one visit he observed the children studying the states and he asked them how many they could name. They came up with about forty names. He jokingly told them that in his day students knew the names of all the states. One lad raised his hand and said, "Yes, but in those days there were only thirteen."

"I've had complaints recently that my sermons are too intellectual," a pastor told his congregation. "That being the case, the following adults are invited to come to the front for today's children's sermon. . . ."

A pastor decided to preach on the Minor Prophets—all twelve of them in a single sermon. Two hours passed and he was only halfway through his message. The congregation became more and more restless, but the people kept their seats.

After four hours, to everyone's relief, he said, "Finally. . ." But to the people's horror, the preacher said, "Oh my goodness—I forgot about Micah! What shall we do with Micah?"

An elderly lady in the front row could take no more. She stood up and announced, "Hey, pastor—Micah can take my seat. I'm going home!"

A preacher was rather proud of his oratorical skills, but his congregation rarely responded to his best lines and flourishes.

After a Sunday morning service, he was frustrated by the people's seeming lack of interest in his talents.

"Today," he fumed to his wife, "I preached to a congregation of fools!"

"So is that why," she asked, "you kept calling them 'beloved brethren'?"

The pastor wasn't known for preaching the best sermons and his congregation finally asked him to move on. The pastor begged for one more chance, which was granted.

The next Sunday, the pastor delivered the clearest, most compelling sermon he'd ever preached. The head deacon caught up to the preacher afterward and suggested he not only stay but receive an increase in salary.

"That was the finest sermon I've ever heard," the deacon said. "But please explain one thing to me. As you began, you raised two fingers on your left hand.

When you finished, you raised two fingers on your right hand. What did those gestures mean?"

"Ah, that," the pastor replied. "Those were the quotation marks."

A pastor commented from the pulpit that he generally prepared his Sunday sermon in the time it took him to walk from the parsonage to the church. Soon, the congregation had bought him a new house ten miles from the church.

Deacons

ALTAR EGO by Len Jones

"Pastor, we appreciate your efforts in fund raising, however, renting the Baptismal Pool out as a Holy Hot Tub during the week is just not acceptable!"

A highly qualified pastoral candidate was trying to impress a skeptical search committee. To do so, he described his extensive educational background, showed an impressive portfolio of sermons and writings, and produced a lengthy list of glowing recommendations from seminary professors, former parishioners, and fellow pastors. Still struggling to get a positive response, the candidate asked the search committee to accompany him to a nearby pond, where he proceeded to walk on the water.

"Humph," grumbled the head deacon. "So I see you can't swim."

✚ ✚ ✚

A pulpit committee had invited a young candidate to interview for the head pastor's position. The committee chairperson asked, "Son, do you know the Bible pretty well?"

"Yes, pretty well," the candidate replied.

"Which part do you know best?" the chairperson asked.

"I know the New Testament best," was the response.

"Which part of the New Testament?" the chairperson persisted.

The young minister shifted in his seat and said nervously, "Uh, several parts."

Nodding, the chairperson asked, "Why don't you tell us the story of the Prodigal Son?"

The candidate cleared his throat and began: "There was a man of the Pharisees named Nicodemus, who went down to Jericho by night and he fell upon stony ground and the thorns choked him half to death. The next morning Solomon and his wife, Gomorrah, came by, and carried him down to the ark for Moses to take care of. But as he was going through the Eastern Gate into the ark, he caught his hair in a limb and he hung there forty days and forty nights. He was starving, but the ravens came and fed him. The next day, the three wise men came and carried him down to the boat dock and he caught a ship to Nineveh. And when he got there he found Delilah sitting on the wall. He said, "Throw her down, boys, throw her down." And they said, "How many times shall we throw her down, till seven times seven?" And he said, "Nay, but seventy times seven." And they threw her down four hundred and ninety times. She burst asunder in their midst and they picked up twelve baskets of the leftovers. And in the resurrection, whose wife shall she be?"

The chairperson interrupted the young minister. "I've heard enough! Let's ask the church to call him as our minister—he's awfully young, but he sure does know his Bible!"

Going over the church finances, the head deacon found a receipt from a local paint store signed by someone named Christian. The deacon hadn't approved buying any paint, so he called the store to point out its mistake.

"I'm sorry," the deacon told the manager, "but there are no Christians here at First Church!"

"YOU MIGHT WATCH YOUR TIME SUNDAY. I THINK
THE DEACONS ARE UP TO SOMETHING."

✛ ✛ ✛

A deacon walked into the pastor's office.

"Pastor," the deacon said, "my wife sent me here to ask if you've seen the invitations you had printed and sent for the Christmas musical?"

"No," the pastor replied. "We were short on time so I sent the secretary to the printer's and told her to have them mailed out immediately."

"Well," the deacon grumbled, "they printed the whole thing backward and we've just invited the entire town to see a musical called 'Leon, Leon'!"

✛ ✛ ✛

The deacons called a meeting with the youth pastor to go over the budget and the youth schedule for the year.

"Well, the kids are off school on Presidents' Day and we're planning a party so we'll need at least seventy-five dollars to fund that," the youth pastor said.

"Presidents' Day?" one of the deacons exclaimed. "Lincoln was known to have walked miles and miles to borrow books and make it to school to get the most basic form of education. So what do they do on his birthday? Close the schools!"

✛ ✛ ✛

An overworked deacon of finances was behind in all of his paperwork. Mountains of receipts and budgets stared back at him from his desk.

"It's a good thing God created the world thousands of years ago," he muttered. "If He did it today, instead of resting on the seventh day, He'd be doing paperwork!"

✝ ✝ ✝

A heated discussion was going on during a meeting of the deacons over the finances. One deacon said to the other: "You just don't know what you're talking about!"

The other deacon, wanting to have the last word on the matter, said, "Well, maybe I don't know what I'm talking about, but if I did know what I was talking about, I'd be right!"

✝ ✝ ✝

"I've got some advice for you," said the deacon to the pastor.

The pastor replied, "The trouble with your advice is that it usually interferes with my plans!"

✝ ✝ ✝

"At least the pastor always has a surprise ending!" the deacon said after another long sermon.

"Yeah," his wife said. "Just when you think it will never end. . .it does!"

✝ ✝ ✝

One of the deacons was in charge of hiring the new secretary. During the interview he asked one woman if she could write shorthand.

"Sure, I can write shorthand," she replied. "It just takes a little longer."

"I don't mind that the deacon always had the last word," the pastor said to his wife after the meeting. "It's waiting for it that I don't care for! That deacon can say more in a look than I can in a sermon!"

The head deacon announced during a board meeting that admission to the church carnival would be five dollars per person. "However," he said, "if someone is over fifty-five, the price will only be $4.50."

From the back of the room, a woman's voice spoke up: "Do you really think I'd give you that information for only fifty cents?"

Q: How many deacons does it take to change a light-bulb?
A: Five. One to actually change the bulb and four to say how much they liked the old one.

During Sunday morning worship, the pastor was so overwhelmed with passion that he dropped to his knees and said, "Before You, Lord, I am nothing."

Not to be outdone, the head deacon also got down on his knees, and said, "Before You, Lord, I am nothing."

Moved by their humility, an usher stepped into the aisle. He fell down on his knees and said, "Before You, Lord, I am nothing."

The deacon noticed the layman and elbowed the pastor. "Look who thinks he's nothing," he whispered.

The pastor answered his phone:

"Hello, is this the pastor?"

"It is."

"This is the IRS. Can you help us with something?"

"I'll try."

"Do you know John Williams?"

"I do."

"Is he a deacon at your church?"

"He is."

"Did he donate $6,000?"

"He will."

Two deacons were discussing which of them was more spiritual.

"Well," said the first, "I'll bet you fifty dollars you can't even repeat the Lord's Prayer."

"I'll take that bet!" said the second. He cleared his throat and began: "Now I lay me down to sleep, I pray the Lord my soul to keep, if I should die before I wake, I pray the Lord my soul to take. Amen."

"Wow," the first deacon said in surprise. "I didn't think you could do it. Here's your fifty dollars!"

An elderly man in the hospital recovering from heart surgery received a visit from one of his church's deacons. The deacon brought flowers and greetings and told the man that they all prayed for him to recover soon and hoped to see him back in church. The elderly man thanked him and said how nice it was for the deacon to stop by.

"It's more than 'nice'!" the deacon said. "It was an official motion! It passed by a vote of twelve to five."

The following was overheard at the deacons' meeting: "We are going to continue to have meetings every day until we find out why no work is getting done."

The deacons were introducing the newest member of the staff to the congregation. A little tongue-tied, the head deacon said, "We passed over a lot of good people to get the one we hired."

Planning to hire extra help for children's ministries over the summer, the deacon made this announcement to the church: "We're only hiring one intern this year and we won't start interviewing candidates for that position until the pastor's daughter finishes her summer classes."

A Methodist preacher met three Baptist deacons on the golf course and the group became friends. A short time later the preacher invited them to visit his church some Sunday and come for dinner afterward. A few weeks later, the three men showed up at the Methodist church. Attendance was good that Sunday and there wasn't a pew available. Several families were already seated on folding chairs. The pastor had just started the service when he saw the three Baptist deacons enter. He leaned down from the pulpit and whispered to one of his own deacons, "Can you get three chairs for my Baptist friends in the back?"

The deacon was hard of hearing and said, "I beg your pardon?"

"Please get three chairs for my Baptist friends," said the preacher.

The deacon leaned in closer with a puzzled look still on his face.

Once more the preacher said: "Three chairs. For the Baptists," he enunciated slowly.

The deacon's face lit up in comprehension, and he stood to face the congregation.

"All right, everybody," he called out to the crowd. "Three cheers for the Baptists!"

The preacher had just finished his Sunday morning sermon and was headed to the deacons' meeting. He went and sat down at the table and the president of the board asked him how he thought the church service went.

The preacher shrugged and said, "The music was

BROTHER BLOOPER'S SECRET TO PICKING UP SPARES

excellent, and I think the prayer and communion times were worshipful, but I just don't think the sermon ever got off the ground."

"Well, it sure did taxi long enough!" the deacon replied.

A young man, fresh out of a northern seminary, had taken his first pastorate in rural Kentucky. For his initial sermon, he preached on the evils of smoking.

After the message, the head deacon pulled the pastor aside and said, "You know, you might want to go easy on the smoking issue. Many in our congregation grow tobacco for a living." The pastor thanked the deacon for his insight.

The next week, the young preacher spoke out against alcohol. Again, the head deacon pulled him aside and said, "You know, you might want to go easy on the drinking issue. Many in our congregation work for the big distillery down the road." Once again, the pastor thanked the deacon for his insight.

On his third Sunday, the new pastor preached against the vice of gambling. And once again, the head deacon pulled him aside to say, "You know, you might want to go easy on the gambling issue. Many in our congregation breed racehorses." A bit flustered now, the pastor again thanked the deacon for his insight.

The next week, the new minister preached on the evils of fishing in another nation's territorial waters.

✢ ✢ ✢

The deacon was nearly deaf but also energetic and helpful. The church was selling new hymnals and it was his particular duty to collect the money from the congregation. During the announcements that Sunday, the preacher announced: "All of you who have children who would like to be dedicated, please bring them to church next Sunday."

The deacon assumed that the pastor was making an announcement about the hymnals and stood up to add, "All of you who don't have any yet, just find me after church and I'll give you as many as you want for five dollars apiece."

"What did you think of the sermon this week?" a new pastor asked one of the deacons.

"It was very insightful, Pastor," the deacon replied. "We didn't really know what sin was until you came here."

"How are things going, Pastor?" the deacon asked.

"Oh, I'm still a little long-winded, I guess," replied the pastor. "I don't mind when I see people checking their watches during the sermon, but it really bothers me when they hold them up to their ears to make sure they're still ticking!"

✟ ✟ ✟

A preacher asked one of his elder deacons to preach while he was away on vacation. When he returned, he ran into a member of his congregation.

"How was church on Sunday?" the preacher asked.

"Oh, we missed you," the church member replied. "We like the deacon a lot as a person, but his message wasn't good at all."

Later in the week, the pastor called the deacon to get his perspective on how things went while he was away.

"Oh the message went fine on Sunday," the deacon replied. "I just used the notes from one of your old sermons."

✟ ✟ ✟

"That was a really long sermon today, Pastor," a deacon commented after the service.

"Well, the clock on the back wall quit working," replied the pastor. "So I didn't realize how much time I was taking!"

"But there was a calendar back there!" replied the deacon.

Missionaries

ALTAR EGO™ by Len Jones

"I WAS JUST FINE WITH THE CONCEPT OF SHARING MY FAITH UNTIL PASTOR SAID WE ACTUALLY HAD TO TALK TO PEOPLE."

A preacher and his choir director were visiting one of their missionaries on the foreign field when the group was suddenly captured by terrorists. The ministers were informed that they were about to be shot.

The preacher exclaimed, "We are men of God! You must let us go!"

When the terrorists refused, the preacher asked the terrorists for one last request each and the terrorists agreed.

The preacher said, "I will give a two-hour sermon in the hopes of saving your souls. And no one is allowed to fall asleep."

The choir director said, "I will give a two-hour concert of my favorite hymns."

"And what about you?" the terrorists asked the missionary.

"Oh, please!" he begged. "Just shoot me first!"

"I was born in Africa," said the child of a missionary.

"What part?" the Sunday school teacher asked.

"All of me!" she replied.

The child of a missionary was attending a liberal school in Europe. On the first day of school, the child's teacher introduced herself as an atheist. She asked the children how many atheists were in the class. Not too sure what atheism was but wanting the teacher's approval, all of the children raised their hands except the missionary kid.

"Do you know what an atheist is?" the teacher asked the missionary kid.

"Yes, I do," the child replied.

"Then why aren't you one?" the teacher asked.

"Because I'm a Christian and I believe in God."

The teacher, noticeably upset, then asked the child why she is a Christian.

"My parents are missionaries and I was brought up knowing all about God and how He sent his Son to save us. My mom is a Christian, and my dad is a Christian, and I am a Christian, too."

The teacher was now quite angry. "That's not a good reason," she shouted. "What if your mom was a fool and your dad was a fool? What would that make you?"

The child shrugged his shoulders and replied, "Then I'd be an atheist."

✛ ✛ ✛

At a special evening church service to highlight missions, a wealthy man rose to give his testimony.

"I'm a billionaire," he said, "and I give all the thanks to God for blessing me so richly."

He continued by telling how, with the first twenty dollars he had earned as a young boy, he attended a similar service at church one night and heard a missionary speak about the work of the Lord in the world. He felt like he needed to give all that he had to God's work so he gave his entire twenty dollars to the Lord.

"I believe God poured out His blessings on me after I made that decision," the rich man continued, "and that is why I am a billionaire today."

Everyone was clearly moved by this man's story. As he walked back to sit down in the pew, an elderly woman leaned over and said, "That was a touching story. . .but now I dare you to do it again!"

A nurse took a short-term mission trip to Africa to help in a medical clinic and share the love of Christ with the sick. One day the African women began to sing a beautiful song full of rich harmony. The nurse was deeply moved and wanted to remember this moment forever. With tears flowing down her face, she turned to her friend and asked, "Can you translate this song for me? I would like to write down the words so I can remember this moment."

Her friend looked at her and replied, "'If you boil the water, you won't get a disease.'"

Some missionaries were back in the United States gaining support for their ministry. As they visited different churches, they would stay in the homes of gracious church members. One night they were staying in the home of a couple with young children. Their six-year-old was entertaining everyone by reading her favorite books aloud. She was just finishing her story when she noticed the family Bible on the mantel.

"What book is that?" the little girl asked her mother.

"That's God's book, honey!" her mother responded with a nervous laugh. "You know that!"

"Well, no one around here ever reads it," the girl said. "Don't you think we ought to give it back?"

✢ ✢ ✢

You know your parents are missionaries when. . .

- you're not sure how to answer the question "Where are you from?"
- you have a passport but not a driver's license.
- you watch travel shows on TV and recognize someone you know.
- you have never played a video game.
- you measure with grams, meters, and liters.
- you receive peanut butter and toothpaste from your grandparents for Christmas.
- you have friends in twenty-five different countries.
- you can speak three languages but can't spell any of them.
- your life story includes paragraphs that start with "Then we went to. . ."
- you're not bothered by eating cooked bugs.

"WHERE I'M FROM IN THE SOUTH, WE DEFINE A MISSIONARY AS A PREACHER WHO'S GONE SO FAR FROM HOME HE CAN'T ORDER GRITS FOR BREAKFAST."

- you find yourself saying, "I don't know, I was out of the country."
- you flew in an airplane six times before your first birthday.
- you have a time-zone map taped to your cell phone.
- you say your prayers in another language.
- you aren't sure *where* home is.
- people you don't ever remember meeting pinch your cheeks and say they remember you when you were tiny.
- people ask for your advice about airline travel.
- you actually know what the term "furlough" means.
- you know that "furlough" doesn't mean you're going on vacation, it means you are stuffed with American food each night and go to bed exhausted from telling the same story over and over again.
- you've spoken from the pulpit a million times but aren't a pastor.
- you ration your peanut butter because you know you won't get your favorite kind again until Christmas.
- you have an abnormal appreciation for your postal carrier.
- you're a little afraid to ask what you're eating, but you eat it with a smile no matter what.
- you are comfortable speaking to any group of people in any part of the world.
- you wince whenever people mispronounce a foreign word.
- you would rather eat seaweed than meatloaf.
- you tell people where you're from and they don't believe you.
- you can't remember the names of the people you were with the entire summer.

- you only get to see your grandparents every two years.
- you love eating rice for every meal.
- walking a mile through the jungle to get to school is normal.
- your family works in the tropics but goes to the States for vacation.
- all music and preaching sounds better to you under a tin roof.
- you don't like American chain coffeehouses because you know what *real* coffee tastes like!
- none of your best friends speaks English.
- you think it's normal to play "football" in the streets with a round, black and white ball.
- you think living in the same house for more than a year is strange.
- the fruit in your lunchbox came from your backyard.
- your school gets cancelled often due to flash floods and mudslides.
- you watch a foreign film and actually know what they are saying without reading the subtitles.

When a young man signed on with a mission agency, the president reminded him that he now must *act* like a missionary.

The recruit was troubled and asked the president, "You know I have a girlfriend. Can I still kiss her good-bye at the airport?"

The president thought for a moment and said, "You may kiss her—if you kiss her the same way you kiss your mother."

The young man paused and then asked, "Can I warn my mother first?"

A missionary to Europe was knocking on doors in his adopted country. At one house, an older woman answered—and when she realized the man was a missionary, she angrily demanded that he leave, slamming the door in his face.

The door, however, bounced back open, and the woman shouted, "Get your foot out of my door!"

"But ma'am. . ." the missionary began, when the woman slammed the door again. Once again, it bounced back open.

"I said, get your foot out of my door!" the woman yelled again. One more time, she slammed the door, only to see it bounce back.

"But ma'am. . ." the missionary said again, only to be cut off.

"Don't talk back to me!" the woman screamed in a rage. "I want you off my property!" She slammed the door a fourth time, only to see it bounce open a fourth time.

"Ma'am!" the missionary yelled, "you'll be able to close your door if you move your cat out of the way!"

✛ ✛ ✛

A pioneer missionary in the jungles of Africa comes upon a lost civilization. He soon realizes that everywhere he goes he hears the beat of drums in the distance.

After two years of hard work, he finally deciphers the tribe's language and approaches the chief with a question.

"Honored sir, everywhere I go here I hear drums beating. Why do you play the drums all the time?"

The chief responds gravely, "If drums stop, terrible

disaster will come."

Puzzled, the missionary asks, "What disaster? A flood, earthquake, disease?"

The chief shakes his head sadly and says, "Worse! If drums stop, bagpipes begin!"

A man was traveling on a short-term missions team to France. Proud of his high-school French skills, he promptly initiated a conversation with a couple on a Paris street corner.

The locals, however, did not answer his questions—and actually stepped back from him, talking together in low tones.

The man approached the missions team leader, saying, "I don't get it. What are they talking about?"

"They're debating," the leader answered, "whether you were speaking English or German."

A pastor went to Venezuela for the first time. He was struggling with the language and didn't understand a whole lot of what was going on. Intending to visit one of the local churches, he got lost but eventually got back on track and found the place. Having arrived late, the church was already packed. The only pew left was in the front row.

So as not to make a fool of himself, he decided to imitate the man sitting next to him. When the man clapped his hands, the pastor clapped, too. When the man stood up to pray, the pastor stood up, too.

The pastor didn't understand a word of the sermon.

When he surmised that the announcements were being read and people were clapping, including the man sitting next to him, the pastor clapped, too.

Then he saw the man next to him stand up. So he stood up, too. Suddenly a hush fell over the entire congregation. A few people gasped. He looked around and saw that nobody else was standing. So he sat down.

After the service, the preacher stood at the door shaking the hands of those who were leaving. When the pastor stretched out his hand to greet him, the preacher said in English, "I take it you don't speak Spanish."

The pastor replied, "No I don't. It's that obvious?"

"Well, yes," said the preacher. "I announced that a baby boy had arrived and would the proud father please stand up."

A missionary to Africa heard of a native who had multiple wives, and decided to confront the man.

"This is against God's laws," the missionary explained. "You need to tell all but one of your women that they can no longer live in your house or call you their husband."

The native thought for a moment. "I wait here," he finally said. "You tell."

✚ ✚ ✚

A young man's first missionary experience was in a leper colony. Though he had great compassion for the people, he dreaded acquiring the disease himself. Having learned that a loss of feeling in the limbs was an early sign of leprosy, he developed a habit of pinching his own legs. If he felt pain, he was reassured.

On furlough back in the States, he was seated at a dinner next to an attractive young woman. Enjoying the conversation, he briefly forgot his fear of leprosy—but then his mind returned to the disease and he surreptitiously reached under the table to pinch his leg.

Not feeling anything, he pinched again, harder this time. But there was still no sensation.

"Oh, no!" he blurted out. "I've got it!"

"Got what?" others at the table asked, concerned.

"Leprosy!" he moaned.

"How do you know that?" another asked.

"One of the early signs is loss of feeling in the legs," he answered. "I've just pinched my leg twice and didn't feel a thing!"

"Oh, don't worry," the young woman responded. "That was *my* leg you were pinching."

In the Pews

ALTAR EGO by Len Jones

"DAD SAYS IF IT WASN'T FOR YOUR SERMONS, HE'D NEVER GET ANY SLEEP."

One Sunday, Mrs. Dunn decided to visit a new church. The sermon seemed to go on and on and a few people in the congregation fell asleep.

After the service, to be friendly, she approached a sleepy-looking gentleman, extended her hand, and said, "Hello—I'm Gladys Dunn."

"You're not the only one," the man replied. "I'm glad it's done, too!"

A young man stood staring at a large plaque hanging on the wall of the church foyer. When the minister approached him, the young man asked, "Sir, what is this?"

"Those are the names of the men who died in the service," the pastor replied.

The two stood quietly before the plaque for a moment. Then the young man broke the silence. "Which service? The 8:30 or the 10:30?"

A young couple was talking to a pastor about joining his church. The minister asked from what church they were transferring their membership. When the young man hesitated, his wife spoke up for him: "From the municipal golf course."

After telling his congregation that the church budget was a bit strained, a pastor asked the people to prayerfully consider giving a little extra in the morning offering. To encourage participation, the minister suggested that whoever gave the most would be allowed to select three hymns.

After the offering had been collected, the pastor glanced down and noticed a one-thousand-dollar bill in one of the plates. He was so excited that he immediately told the congregation that he wanted to personally thank the donor.

When an elderly woman in the back shyly raised her hand, the pastor asked her to join him in the front of the sanctuary. She slowly made her way to the platform, where the minister commended her generosity. Then he encouraged her to pick out three hymns.

The woman's eyes brightened. Looking over the congregation, she pointed to the three most handsome men, saying, "I'll take him. . .and him. . .and him!"

During morning announcements, the pastor mentioned that a woman's watch had been found in the restroom. The timepiece, he said, could be claimed by anyone providing an adequate description.

Then the song leader announced the next hymn: "Lord, Her Watch Thy Church Is Keeping."

Congregants looked at each other in confusion when the pastor announced that the church's "Prison Quartet" would be singing next. "You know," he explained, "they're behind a few bars and always looking for the key."

Church leaders announced a new fundraiser to benefit the missions program. "We'll be starting a new bowling league," an elder said. "We're looking for members, as well as a team name."

Someone shouted out, "How about the Holy Rollers?"

The pastor had come to realize that, during the congregational scripture reading, one woman read the verses much faster than the other church members. So one morning, he made an announcement: "As we read Psalm 23 in unison, will the woman who is 'by still waters' while the rest of us are 'in green pastures' please wait while we catch up?"

A boy knelt beside his bed to say his prayers with his mother and grandmother.

"Dear God," he said softly, "please bless Mommy and Daddy and all the family and please give me a good night's sleep." Then he looked up and shouted, "And don't forget to give me a bicycle for my birthday!"

Surprised, his mother said, "There's no need to shout like that. . . . God isn't deaf."

"No," the boy replied, "but Grandma is."

✛ ✛ ✛

After a church service, three boys were bragging about their fathers.

The first boy said, "My dad scribbles a few words on a piece of paper, calls it a poem, and gets fifty dollars for it."

The second boy said, "That's nothing—my dad scribbles a few words on a piece of paper, calls it a song, and he gets a hundred dollars."

The third boy said, "I've got you both beat. My dad scribbles a few words on a piece of paper, calls it a sermon, and it takes four people to collect all the money!"

✛ ✛ ✛

A four-year-old boy was asked to return thanks before Christmas dinner. He began his prayer by thanking God for all his friends, naming them one by one. Then he thanked God for his mommy, his daddy, his brother and sister, his grandma, his grandpa, and all his aunts and uncles. Then he began to thank God for the food.

The boy gave thanks for the turkey, the dressing, the cranberry sauce, the pies, the cakes, and even the whipped cream. Then he paused. After a long silence, he looked up at his mother and asked, "If I thank God for the broccoli, won't He know that I'm lying?"

"YOU KIDS WIPE THOSE GRINS OFF YOUR FACES. . .
YOU'RE IN CHURCH!"

A young boy was acting up during the morning worship service. His parents did their best to maintain some sense of order in the pew, but they were losing the battle. Finally, the father grabbed the boy and began carrying him toward the exit. Just before reaching the foyer, the little one called loudly to the congregation, "Y'all pray for me, now!"

After church, a little girl sat outside the building crying. When her older brother came out the door and noticed her in tears, he asked her what was wrong.

"The pastor talked about the sin of vanity today." She sniffled. "I've been sinning a lot—every day I look in the mirror and tell myself how pretty I am."

"Oh that's not a sin," the brother responded. "That's a mistake!"

When they would travel together on long trips, the young boy's mother would always tell him to go to sleep so that the trip would be over with quicker. One weekend the mother and son traveled to his grandparents' house several states away and they joined them for church that Sunday. The sermon was very long and his mother looked over to find her son asleep. She nudged him to wake up.

"But Mom, I'm trying to get this over with quicker!" he replied.

A father asked his little boy if he knew how a person gets saved.

"We'll be saved by going to our church every Sunday," the boy said without hesitation.

His father explained that going to their church each week would not save them.

"Well, then, we better find another church!" replied the boy.

A family had the pastor over for dinner after church. They asked their five-year-old son if he would say the blessing.

"God is great, God is good," the child began, "thank You for this food. But I would thank You even more if Mommy lets us have ice cream for dessert. And liberty and justice for all!"

+ + +

A young mother was having an awful time trying to get her squirming six-year-old to be quiet during church. Halfway through the sermon she had an idea. She leaned over and whispered to her son, "If you don't hush up and listen, the pastor is going to lose his place and have to start his sermon all over again!"

"WE REALIZE THAT NOT EVERYONE IS FOR THIS MOTION, BUT LET'S ALL TRY TO KEEP AN OPEN MIND AS WE HEAR THE PRESENTATION."

A young girl was sitting on her grandfather's lap as he read her a bedtime story. Every so often she would reach up to touch his wrinkled cheek. Then she would touch her own cheek and then his again. There was obviously something on her mind.

"Papa," she asked finally, "did God make you?"

"Yes, sweetie," he answered, "God made me a long, long time ago."

"Did God make me, too?" she asked.

"He certainly did, honey," her grandpa replied. "God made you just a little while ago."

After touching his cheek and then her own again, she concluded, "God's getting better at it, isn't He?"

After church one Sunday, a young boy walked up to the pastor. "Pastor," he said, "I heard you say in church that our bodies came from the dust."

"That's right, son, I did."

"And didn't you say that when we die, our bodies go back to dust?"

"Yes, I'm glad you were listening," the pastor replied. "Why do you ask?"

"Well I think you better come over to our house right away and look under my bed," the boy said, " 'cause there's someone either coming or going!"

On Sunday morning, during the pastor's prayer, a shrill whistle came from a young boy sitting in a pew. His mother was horrified and quickly hushed him into silence.

After church, the mother asked, "Whatever possessed you to make such a terrible noise in church?"

"Well," he answered, "I've been asking God to teach me to whistle. . .and just then, He did!"

As a young boy thumbed through an old family Bible, something fell out from between the pages. It was an old leaf that had been pressed in the book for years.

"Grandma," he called out, "look what I found!"

"What do you have there, dear?" his grandmother asked.

In astonishment, the boy replied, "I think it's Adam's suit!"

An elderly woman was ready to hand down an old family Bible to her only grandchild. Excited, the young girl asked a number of questions, both about the family members whose births and deaths were recorded in the Bible and about various aspects of the scripture itself. The older woman was trying to keep up with the child's questions, answering in terms she could understand, until the youngster asked, "Which virgin was the mother of Jesus? Was it the virgin Mary, or the King James virgin?"

✛ ✛ ✛

Three brothers left home, started careers, and prospered. During a dinner together, they discussed the gifts they were giving their mother for her seventy-fifth birthday.

The first brother commented, "I built a big house for Mom."

The second said, "I sent her an expensive car with a driver."

The third brother reported, "You remember how Mom enjoys reading the Bible? Well, since she doesn't see so well anymore, I sent her a remarkable parrot that recites the scripture. It took elders in the church twelve years to teach him the whole Bible. Mom just has to name the chapter and verse and the parrot will say it."

Soon, the woman sent letters of thanks to her sons. To the first she penned, "The house you built me is nice—but way too big. I live in just one room, but I still have to clean the whole place."

To the second she wrote, "The car is beautiful, but I really don't enjoy traveling anymore. And, besides, that driver drives way too fast!"

Finally, she wrote to the third, "Thank you so much for your wonderful gift. That little chicken you sent was delicious!"

Girl: "Grandma, were you on Noah's ark?"

Grandma: "Of course not, dear!"

Girl: "Then how did you survive the flood?"

✛ ✛ ✛

A man was praying. "Lord, how long is a million years to You?"

"Only a second," came God's reply.

"And Lord, how much is a million dollars to You?" the man asked.

"Only a penny," God answered.

"Then Lord," the man prayed, "may I have a penny?"

"Of course," God replied. "Just a second."

✛ ✛ ✛

A man was praying.

"Lord," he said, "it's been a good day so far. I haven't been in any fights, stolen anything, boasted, or looked at a pretty woman. But now comes the big test, and I'm begging for your help: I'm going to get out of bed and get ready for work. . . ."

✛ ✛ ✛

A church member had arrived a few minutes early for his pastoral counseling session. So, he sat outside the office clapping his hands in a rhythmic pattern: *clap. . .clap-clap-clap. . .clap-clap.*

When the pastor invited the man into his office, he asked, "And what's the hand clapping all about?"

"It's a secret ritual," the man answered. "I learned it from a street musician."

"What does it do?" the pastor asked.

"It keeps killer sharks away," the man replied.

"Oh, you don't need to worry about sharks in my office," the pastor said with a smile.

"Thanks to me," the man answered.

"IF ALL THE PEOPLE WHO SLEPT IN CHURCH WERE LAID END TO END. . .AT LEAST THEY WOULD BE COMFORTABLE!"

A pastor was visiting with a couple when their young son ran into the house, holding a mouse by its tail.

"Don't worry, Mom, it's dead!" the boy shouted. "We chased him, then we hit him—"

At that point, the boy noticed the minister sitting at the table, and lowered his voice to conclude, ". . .until the Lord called him home."

A mother found her five-year-old son coating his hand with lotion before church.

"What on earth are you doing?" she asked her son.

"I'm getting my shaking hand ready!" he replied.

Suggested pick-up lines for church:
- "Is this pew taken?"
- "Excuse me, but I think you're sitting on my Bible."
- "Worship here often?"

As the pastor greeted his congregation at the door after the service, a woman told him, "Pastor, that was a very good sermon."

Modestly, the preacher replied, "Oh, I have to give the credit to the Holy Spirit."

"Well," she answered, "it wasn't *that* good!"

Sunday School

"WELL, NO, BRANDON, I DON'T THINK THE BIBLE TELLS US WHETHER SAMSON COULD BEAT UP SPIDERMAN. BUT I'M SURE HE COULD HAVE!"

A Sunday school teacher asked the children to say how they would feel if Jesus were looking right at them. One four-year-old raised his hand and said he would feel "toasty and nice!"

A Sunday school teacher was telling her class the story of the Good Samaritan, in which a man was beaten, robbed, and left for dead. She described the situation in vivid detail so her students would better understand the drama. Then she asked the class, "If you saw someone lying on the roadside wounded and bleeding, what would you do?"

One little girl said, "I think I'd throw up!"

A young boy stunned his parents when he began to empty his pockets of nickels, dimes, and quarters.

"Where did you get all that money?" his mother asked nervously.

"At Sunday school," the boy replied. "They have bowls of it."

Finding one of her Sunday school kids making faces at others on the playground, the teacher stopped to gently reprove the child. Smiling sweetly, the Sunday school teacher said, "When I was a child, I was told that if I made ugly faces, my face would freeze and I would stay like that."

The boy looked up at her and replied, "Well, you can't say you weren't warned."

A Sunday school teacher asked her young class as they were on the way to church service, "Why is it necessary to be quiet in church?"

A little girl replied, "Because people are sleeping."

A seven-year-old was overheard reciting the Lord's Prayer during Sunday school: "And forgive us our trash passes as we forgive those who passed trash against us."

A mother was teaching her six-year-old the Lord's Prayer. For several evenings at bedtime she repeated it after her mother. One night she said she was ready to say it all by herself. The mother was impressed to hear her daughter as she carefully enunciated each word, right up to the end of the prayer. "Lead us not into temptation," she prayed, "but deliver us some e-mail, Amen."

The Sunday school teacher asked if any of her students would like to say a prayer. One little girl was willing and began her prayer like this: "Our Father, who art in heaven, hello! What be Thy name?"

A seven-year-old girl who was trying to cope with
Sunday school and first grade at the same time came up
with this interesting blend of things she had just learned:
"Give us this day our daily bread, and liberty and justice
for all."

"Can you complete this sentence?" the teacher asked
her Sunday school class after learning the Lord's Prayer.
"Give us this day our. . ."

"Jelly bread!" one little boy exclaimed.

"Can anyone recite the beginning of the Lord's Prayer?"
the teacher asked.

One Sunday school student said, "Our Father who
art in heaven, Hollywood be Thy name."

At the end of Sunday school, the teacher asked if any of
her six-year-olds would like to say a closing prayer. The
preacher's son stood and bowed his head. He prayed:
"For thine is the kingdom, and the power, and the glory,
forever and ever, AM and FM."

After learning the Lord's Prayer in Sunday school, one little boy kissed his mommy and his new baby brother. "Mommy," he asked, "if God gives us our daily bread, and Santa brings us presents, and the stork brings babies. . .why do we need Daddy around?"

A Sunday school teacher asked her students to take some time on Sunday afternoon to write a letter to God. They were to bring their letters back the following Sunday. One little boy wrote, "Dear God, we had a good time at church today. Wish You could have been there." Another little boy wrote, "Dear God, thank You for my baby brother, but I prayed for a puppy." A little girl wrote: "Dear God, if You watch me in church on Sunday, I'll show You my new shoes!" Another interesting letter came from a young girl. "Dear God," she wrote, "please send me a real live pony. I promise I never asked for anything before. You can look it up."

A child came home from Sunday school and told his mother that they sang a new song about a cross-eyed bear named Gladly. It took his mother awhile before she realized that the hymn was really "Gladly the Cross I'd Bear."

An eight-year-old boy was asked by his mother what he had learned in Sunday school. "Well, Mom, our teacher told us how God sent Moses behind enemy lines on a rescue mission to lead the Israelites out of Egypt. When he got to the Red Sea, he had his engineers build a bridge, and all the people walked across safely. He used his walkie-talkie to radio headquarters and call in an air strike. They sent in bombers to blow up the bridge and all the Israelites were saved!"

"Now, son, is that *really* what your teacher taught you?" his mother asked.

"Well, no, Mom—but if I told it the way the teacher did, you'd never believe it!"

Every evening, a mother and her son knelt down beside his bed so he could say his prayers. One night the little boy said this: "Now I lay me down to sleep, I pray the Lord my soul to keep, if I should die before I wake. . .can I have breakfast with You in the morning?"

A Sunday school teacher asked her class why Joseph and Mary took Jesus with them to Jerusalem. One little girl raised her hand and said, "Because they couldn't get a babysitter."

A little girl asked her Sunday school teacher a question: "If the people of Israel are Israelites, and the people of Canaan are Canaanites, are the people of Paris called Parasites?"

A Sunday school teacher asked her children if anyone knew what the first commandment was. A little boy who was very sure of himself stood and said, "The first commandment was when Eve told Adam to eat the apple."

"Does anyone know what the seventh commandment is?" a Sunday school teacher asked her twelve-year-olds. "The seventh commandment is 'Thou shalt not admit adultery,' " a boy said.

A Sunday school class studying the Ten Commandments was ready to learn the last one. The teacher asked if anyone could tell her what the commandment was. A little boy raised his hand and shouted out, "Thou shall not take the covers off thy neighbor's wife!"

A Sunday school teacher was teaching the Ten Commandments to her preschool class. After explaining the commandment, "Honor thy father and thy mother," she asked, "Is there a commandment that teaches us how to treat our brothers and sisters?"

Without missing a beat one little girl answered, "Thou shalt not kill."

When the Sunday school teacher asked the children what they knew about Moses, she got an interesting answer. One little boy jumped up and shouted, "Moses went up on Mount Cyanide to get the Ten Amendments!"

A Sunday school class was asked to list the Ten Commandments in any order. One child wrote, "3, 6, 1, 8, 4, 5, 9, 2, 10, 7."

"Okay, does anyone else know anything about Moses?" the Sunday school teacher asked.

"Yes, I know," one boy replied. "Moses died before he ever reached Canada."

A Sunday school class was learning all about Joshua and the Hebrews. "Does anyone remember what battle Joshua fought?" the teacher asked.

A little boy shouted, "Joshua fought the battle of Geritol!"

During Sunday school the teacher decided to give a little quiz to her students. She wanted to see if the children would be able to write out the Golden Rule. The teacher walked around the classroom to see how the children were doing. She was pleased to see that many of them got it exactly right. She was shocked, however, to see one little boy's rendition. He had written: "Do one to others before they do one to you."

✜ ✜ ✜

"Does anyone know what the Epistles are?" the Sunday school teacher asked.

"Aren't they the wives of the apostles?" a little girl asked.

✜ ✜ ✜

During Bible quizzing, the Sunday school children were asked to write down everything they knew about the apostle Paul. One boy wrote: "Saint Paul cavorted to Christianity. He preached holy acrimony, which is another name for marriage."

✜ ✜ ✜

A Sunday school teacher asked a little boy, "Do you know who built the ark?"

"No, uh. . . ," he answered quietly.

"That's right!" replied the teacher.

During another Sunday of Bible quizzing, the kids were asked to write down what they knew about Noah. One ten-year-old wrote: "Noah's wife was called Joan of Ark. Noah built an ark, which the animals came onto in pears."

A Sunday school teacher asked, "Do you think Noah did a lot of fishing on the ark?"

"How could he?" one boy answered. "He only had two worms!"

"What happened at the Red Sea?" the Sunday school teacher asked.

A young girl replied, "Moses led the Hebrews there and they made unleavened bread, which is bread without any ingredients."

"Mommy, I learned the greatest miracle in the whole Bible today at Sunday school," an ornery little boy told his mother.

"What was it, son?" his mother asked, expecting to hear about the parting of the Red Sea, the many miracles of Jesus, or the burning bush.

The boy replied, "Joshua told his son to stand still. . . and he obeyed him!"

A Sunday school class was learning about the disciples. The teacher asked if any of the children remembered anything about Matthew. One five-year-old replied, "He was one of the opossums, and he was a taxi man."

A group of middle-school children was learning about Lot during Sunday school. The teacher asked the students why Lot's wife was in so much trouble. One boy answered, "It's because she was a pillar of salt by day, but a ball of fire by night."

The Sunday school teacher had just finished the lesson about Lot's wife looking back on Sodom and turning into a pillar of salt. She then asked if anyone had any questions.

A little boy raised his hand and said, "My mommy looked back once when she was driving and she turned into a telephone pole!"

The Sunday school teacher was telling the story of Lot. She read, "The man named Lot was warned to take his wife and flee out of the city, but his wife looked back and was turned into a pillar of salt."

"Well," a little boy asked, "what happened to the flea?"

The Sunday school teacher asked, "Now, tell me, do you say prayers before eating?"

"Nope," the boy replied, "we don't have to. My mom is a good cook!"

Two twelve-year-olds were walking home from Sunday school, each deep in thought. Finally one said, "What do you think of all this stuff about the devil we studied today?"

The other boy replied, "Well, you know how Santa Claus turned out. . .this is probably just your dad, too."

During Sunday school, the teacher asked the children what *Amen* means.

A little boy raised his hand and said, "It means tha–tha–tha–that's all, folks!"

The teacher asked her Sunday school class to draw pictures of their favorite Bible stories. She was puzzled by one little boy's picture that showed four people on an airplane, so she asked him which story it was meant to represent.

"The flight to Egypt," the boy said.

"I see. . .and that must be Mary, Joseph, and baby Jesus," the teacher said. "But who's the fourth person?"

"Oh, that's Pontius the pilot!"

✤ ✤ ✤

A little boy in the Sunday school kindergarten class got up from his craft and went over to ask one of the adult helpers a question.

"Are you a Christian?"

"Yes," she replied.

"Do you read your Bible every day?"

She nodded her head. "Yes, I do."

"Do you pray often?" the boy asked next, and again she answered, "Yes."

With that he asked his final question: "Will you hold my quarter while I go to the bathroom?"

After Sunday school one morning, one of the parents invited the teacher over for dinner along with several other families from the church. At the table, she asked her six-year-old daughter to say the blessing for the meal.

"I don't know what to say," she replied.

"Just say what you hear Mommy say," her mother said.

The little girl bowed her head and said, "Dear Lord, why on earth did I invite all these people to dinner?"

After Sunday school a little girl went to find her mother in church.

"Mommy," she said, "can we leave now?"

"No," her mother replied.

"Well, I think I have to throw up!" the girl exclaimed.

"Then run back to the bathroom and I'll come check on you in a little while."

After about thirty seconds, the little girl returned to her seat.

"Did you throw up?" her mother asked.

"Yes," the girl replied.

"How could you have gone all the way to the back of the building and gotten back so quickly?"

"I didn't have to go all the way to the back, Mommy. They have a box right next to the front door that says, 'For the Sick.' "

A little girl, dressed in her Sunday best, was running as fast as she could, trying not to be late for Sunday school. As she ran she prayed, "Dear Jesus, please don't let me be late! Dear Jesus, please don't let me be late!"

While she was running and praying, she tripped on a curb and fell, dirtying her dress and tearing her stockings. She got up, brushed herself off, and started running again. Then she began to pray, "Dear Jesus, please don't let me be late. . .but please don't shove me, either!"

A Sunday school teacher was telling how God created everything—including people. One boy seemed especially intent when she described how Eve was created from one of Adam's ribs. Later in the week, his mother noticed him lying down as though he were ill. She asked him, "What's the matter?"

He responded, "I have pain in my side. . .I think I'm going to have a wife."

✛ ✛ ✛

A Sunday school teacher walked around her class, observing the four-year-olds as they drew pictures. She asked one little girl, who was working diligently, about her drawing.

"I'm drawing God," the girl replied.

The teacher paused and then said, "But no one knows what God looks like."

Without looking up, the little girl replied, "They will in a minute."

On Palm Sunday a five-year-old boy had a sore throat and stayed home from church with a babysitter. When the family returned home, they were carrying several palm branches. The boy asked them what they were.

"People held them over Jesus' head as He walked by," his father told him.

"Wouldn't you know it," the boy fumed. "The one Sunday I don't go and Jesus shows up."

On Easter a teacher began her Sunday school lesson by reaching into her bag and pulling out an egg. "Does anyone want to guess what's in here?" she asked.

"I know, I know!" a little boy exclaimed. "Pantyhose!"

"We've been learning how powerful the kings and queens were in Bible times," a Sunday school teacher told her class. "But there is a higher power. Who can tell me what that is?"

One boy shrugged. "Aces?"

The children were lined up for snacks during Sunday school. At the head of the table was a large tray of apples. The teacher wrote a note and posted it on the apple tray: "Take only ONE. God is watching."

Moving along the snack line, at the other end was a large tray of chocolate chip cookies. A girl wrote this note, which she put next to the tray of cookies: "Take all you want. God is watching the apples."

✚ ✚ ✚

It was snack time at Sunday school and the teacher was getting ready to hand out giant chocolate chip cookies. Two young brothers began to argue over who would get the first cookie. The teacher saw an opportunity for a moral lesson: "If Jesus were here, He would say, 'Let my brother have the first cookie. I can wait.' "

The older boy turned to his brother and said, "You be Jesus."

"PASTOR, WHY IS IT THAT THE WORST BEHAVED CHILD ALWAYS HAS THE BEST ATTENDANCE RECORD?"

After a lesson about being good little boys and girls—as Jesus would want them to be—the teacher asked one boy to pray. He stood up and said, "Lord, if You can't make me a better boy, don't worry about it. I'm having a real good time like I am."

After an entire Sunday school class was dedicated one morning, a little boy sobbed all the way home in the backseat of the car. His parents asked him three times what was wrong, before he finally replied, "The preacher said he wanted us brought up in a Christian home—but I just want to stay with you guys."

A Sunday school teacher was using the squirrel as an object lesson on being prepared. "I'm going to describe something," she told the class, "and I want you to raise your hand when you know what it is." The children waited eagerly.

"This thing lives in trees [pause] and eats nuts [pause]." No hands went up.

"It's gray [pause] and has a long bushy tail [pause]." The children looked at each other, but nobody raised a hand.

"And it jumps from branch to branch [pause] and chatters and flips its tail when it's excited [pause]."

Finally one boy tentatively raised his hand. "Well," he said, "I know the answer must be Jesus. . .but it sure sounds like a squirrel to me!"

The Sunday school teacher asked if anyone could name the first man. One little boy promptly answered, "Adam." Then asked to name the first woman, he pondered long and hard before finally suggesting, "Madam?"

A young boy was spending a weekend with his grandmother after a particularly difficult week in kindergarten. On Saturday morning, his grandmother took him to the park to play in the beautiful, newly fallen snow.

"Doesn't it look like an artist painted this scenery?" Grandma asked. "Do you think God painted this just for you?"

"Yes, God did it," the boy answered, "and He did it left-handed."

Confused, Grandma asked, "What makes you think that?"

"Well," said the boy, "we learned at Sunday school last week that Jesus sits on God's right hand!"

A Sunday school teacher encouraged her students to memorize Psalm 23. She gave the children a month to learn the passage, but one little boy just couldn't retain the words. After much practice, he could barely get past the first line. When the day came for the kids to recite the psalm in front of the congregation, the boy was nervous. When he stepped to the microphone, he said, "The Lord is my Shepherd. . .and that's all I need to know!"

✛ ✛ ✛

A Sunday school teacher asked her class, "What was Jesus' mother's name?"

One child answered, "Mary."

"Who knows what Jesus' father's name was?" the teacher asked next.

A little boy replied, "Verge."

"Verge?" the teacher asked. "Where did you hear that?"

"Well," the boy said, "you know they're always talking about Verge 'n' Mary."

✛ ✛ ✛

On a beautiful fall morning, a Sunday school class was taking a nature walk. "Isn't God amazing?" the teacher said. "Look at all the beautiful colors on the leaves!"

"I don't mean to criticize God," a fourth grader said, "but wouldn't He have enjoyed it more if He made the leaves fall *up*?"

✛ ✛ ✛

"What did you do for Thanksgiving?" the teacher asked her preschool class on Sunday.

"We ate a sick turkey!" said one girl.

"A sick turkey?" the teacher asked.

"Yeah," the girl continued. "All afternoon it had a thermometer in it."

✝ ✝ ✝

A Sunday school teacher thought it would be nice for her students to write letters to welcome their new pastor. Here is a sampling of the results:

Dear Pastor,
  I know God loves everybody but He never met my sister.

Dear Pastor,
  My father should have been the new minister instead of you. Every day he gives us a sermon about something.

Dear Pastor,
  I'm sorry I can't leave more money in the plate, but my father didn't give me a raise in my allowance. Could you have a sermon about a raise in my allowance?

Dear Pastor,
  My mother is very religious. She goes to play bingo at church every week even if she has a cold.

Dear Pastor,
  I think a lot more people would come to your church if you moved it to a playground.

Dear Pastor,
  Please say a prayer for our Little League team. We need God's help or a new pitcher.

Dear Pastor,
  My father says I should learn the Ten Commandments. But I don't think I want to because

we have enough rules already in my house.

Dear Pastor,
  I liked your sermon on Sunday. Especially when it was finished.

The Sunday school teacher told her class about the "children of Israel." She described how they crossed the Red Sea, defeated the Philistines in battle, and built the Temple. Then she was interrupted by a curious young girl.
  "What were all the grown-ups doing?" she asked.

A little girl was asked to pray in Sunday school. "Dear Lord," she said, "please take care of my daddy and my mommy and my brother and my doggy and me. And please take care of Yourself, too, Lord. If anything happens to You, we'll all be in big trouble."

A little girl was asked to pray during Sunday school. She hesitated for a moment, then began to recite the alphabet.
  "What are you doing?" the teacher interrupted.
  "I can't think of what to say," the young girl explained. "So I'm just saying all the letters I know and God can put them together however He wants."

A little boy was struggling to recall his lines for a Sunday school presentation. His mother sat in the front row to prompt him, gesturing and forming the words silently with her lips, but to no avail.

Finally, she leaned forward and whispered the cue, "I am the light of the world."

The child beamed and, with great feeling and a loud, clear voice, said, "My mom is the light of the world."

✝ ✝ ✝

Here are some letters from Sunday school students to God:

Dear God,
  Please put another holiday between Christmas and Easter. There is nothing good in there now.

Dear Mr. God,
  I wish You would not make it so easy for people to come apart. I had to have three stitches and a shot.

Dear God,
  I think about You sometimes even when I'm not praying.

Dear God,
  Did You really mean "do unto others as they do unto you"? Because if You did, then I'm going to fix my brother.

Dear God,
  I didn't think orange went with purple until I saw the sunset You made on Tuesday. That was cool!

Dear God,
  I read the Bible. What does "begat" mean? Nobody will tell me.

Dear God,
  Are You really invisible or is that a trick?

Dear God,
  Did You mean for the giraffe to look like that or was it an accident?

Dear God,
Instead of letting people die and having to make new ones, why don't You just keep the ones You have now?

Dear God,
Who draws the lines around countries?

Dear God,
I went to this wedding and they kissed right in church. Is that okay?

Dear God,
Why is Sunday school on Sunday? I thought it was supposed to be our day of rest.

Dear God,
Maybe Cain and Abel would not hate each other so much if they had their own rooms. It works for me and my brother.

Dear God,
I want to be just like my daddy when I get big but not with so much hair all over.

Dear God,
You don't have to worry about me. I always look both ways.

Dear God,
I bet it is very hard for You to love all of everybody in the whole world. There are only four people in our family and I can never do it.

Dear God,
Of all the people who work for You, I like Noah and

David the best.

Dear God,
   My brother told me about being born but it doesn't sound right. They're just kidding, aren't they?

Dear God,
   I would like to live nine hundred years like that guy in the Bible.

Ten Things We Wouldn't Know If There Were No Sunday School:

1. With all eyes closed for prayer, anything can happen in a room full of kids.
2. Prayer requests reveal a lot about parents and home life.
3. Cheap glue adheres to skin and everything else.
4. Helium intoxication does not render respect outside of Sunday school—for instance, in a church staff meeting.
5. Upright pianos are not as sturdy as you might think.
6. Church janitors do not have a sense of humor.
7. When offering money is dropped, it always rolls clear to the other end of the room.
8. There *is* an animal heaven.
9. Parachute games should not be used in rooms with chandeliers or candles.
10. Animal crackers can be sneezed out the nose.

A naughty little boy had been sent to the corner during Sunday school. After a while he approached the teacher, telling her he had thought things over and asked God for help.

"That was wise of you," said the teacher. "I'm sure God heard your prayer and will help you to stop misbehaving."

"Oh, I didn't ask Him to help me," the boy replied. "I asked God to help you put up with me."

✛ ✛ ✛

A young boy really wanted to be Joseph in the Sunday school Christmas play. Instead, the teacher cast him as the innkeeper—and the boy was obviously displeased.

On the night of the play, the children playing Mary and Joseph knocked on the door and asked the boy, as the innkeeper, if he had a room for them at the inn.

"Sure," he replied. "I've got lots of room. Come on in!"

✛ ✛ ✛

A Sunday school teacher asked her young students to explain God. Responses included the following:

"One of God's main jobs is making people. He makes them to replace the ones that die so there will always be enough people to take care of things on our planet. He only makes babies, not grown-ups, because they are small and easier to handle."

✛ ✛ ✛

"God listens to prayers. A whole lot of this goes on because some people, like preachers, pray more than just at bedtime and supper. So that's why God doesn't have any time to listen to the radio or watch TV."

"I know that God hears everything so I think there must be a lot of noise in His ears. But maybe He has thought of a way to turn it off or turn it down."

"God is very busy because He sees everything and hears everything and is everywhere. So you shouldn't waste His time and go over your Mom and Dad's head to ask for something they already said you can't have."

"You should always go to church every Sunday because it makes God happy. It's really important to make God happy. Never skip church so that you can go to the beach or do something else that you think will be more fun. This is wrong! And by the way, the sun doesn't come out at the beach until noon anyway."

"What did you learn in Sunday school today, honey?" a mother asked her son.

"Not enough, I guess," replied the young boy. "They want me to come back again next week!"

A Sunday school teacher was talking about David and

his time in the fields with the sheep. After giving a description, the teacher asked, "Now what does that make David?" She was hoping that someone would answer, "A shepherd."

"Probably only a thousand bucks a year," stated a boy matter-of-factly.

✛ ✛ ✛

"How will you celebrate Easter?" asked the teacher on Sunday.

"We're going to kill a bunch of eggs!" shouted a little girl with excitement.

"What do you mean?" asked the teacher in astonishment.

"Well Mommy says I get to 'die' eggs today," replied the girl.

✛ ✛ ✛

During the children's sermon, the pastor was talking about fishing.

"If you want to catch a fish, what bait should you use?" asked the pastor.

"Worms!" the children yelled.

"Well, what would you use if you wanted to catch men?"

"Fried chicken!" a little girl shouted.

✛ ✛ ✛

A teacher was telling her Sunday school class that God makes trees and vegetables and sunshine and rain.

"God makes everything," said the teacher.

"Well He doesn't make my bed!" shouted one little

boy.

✦ ✦ ✦

A Sunday school teacher was just finishing her lesson when she asked this question to conclude: "Children, what must we do first before we can expect forgiveness for our sins?"

A little boy raised his hand and said, "Well, first we've got to sin."

✦ ✦ ✦

A young boy came in late to Sunday school. He was usually prompt so the teacher asked him if something was wrong. The boy told her that he was planning to go fishing with his dad, but at the last minute his dad told him that he needed to go to church instead.

"Well, I'm glad you came! Did your dad explain to you why it's more important to come to church than go fishing?" asked the teacher.

"Yes," the boy replied, "Dad said he didn't have enough bait for the both of us."

✦ ✦ ✦

"What do we know about God?" asked the Sunday school teacher.

"He's an artist!" said one little boy.

"Really?" replied the teacher. "How do you know?"

"You know! 'Our Father, who does art in heaven'. . ."

142

The teacher was asking her class to name their favorite Bible stories. One child named Daniel in the lions' den, one named David and Goliath, one named Moses parting the Red Sea. But one little boy was stumped. He finally said, "I guess I like the one about the multitude that loafs and fishes."

A young boy came home from church one Sunday with a chocolate ice cream cone. "Where did you get that?" asked his father.

"With the money you gave me this morning," replied the boy.

"But that money was for church!" said his father.

"I know," the boy replied, "but the preacher met me at the door and got me in for free!"

Sunday school teacher: "You missed church last Sunday, didn't you?"

Boy: "No, I didn't miss it at all!"

"Can anyone name the Roman emperor who was the worst persecutor of the early Christians?" a Sunday school teacher asked her fifth- and sixth-graders.

"Nero," one boy quickly answered.

"Yes, that's right," the teacher responded. "And how did he persecute the believers?"

"He tortured them in Rome," the boy replied.

"And do we know how he tortured them?" the

teacher continued.

"He played the violin at 'em," the boy announced.

Sunday school teacher: "What became of Tyre?"

Boy: "The Lord punctured it."

"Who was the first woman?" a Sunday school teacher asked.

Shrugging, a girl responded, "I don't know."

"I'll give you a hint," the teacher said. "It had something to do with an apple."

"Hmm," the girl replied, "Granny Smith?"

"What did we learn from Jonah and the big fish?" a teacher asked her Sunday school class.

"What we learned," a boy spoke up, "is that people make big fish sick."

A young boy ran up to his father after church, saying proudly, "I know what the Bible means!"

" 'What the Bible means?' " the father replied. "I don't understand."

"You know," the boy answered. "*B* stands for basic. *I* stands for instructions. *B* stands for before. *L* stands for leaving. *E* stands for earth."

The Sacraments

"UH-OH, DRIBBLE GLASSES. I KNEW WE SHOULDN'T HAVE ORDERED FROM ACME MAGIC SHOP."

A new pastor in a rural church was offering an invitation.
A young woman came forward during the decision
time, wanting to accept Christ and be baptized. After
sharing the scriptures with her, the pastor took her
down to the "baptizing hole" at the creek and baptized
her. One of the elders came up to the pastor afterward
and expressed his concern over her immersion. When
the pastor asked what he was concerned about he said
that the pastor had not submerged all of the woman
under the water. When asked specifically what part did
not get immersed, he motioned toward his stomach.
The woman he was talking about was eight months'
pregnant. The pastor shrugged it off and told him, "She's
okay, because we don't baptize babies in the New
Testament church."

One communion Sunday, the communion steward prepared an unusual communion. When it came time to
uncover the elements, the grape juice looked darker than
usual. The minister thought nothing of it and began to
serve the communion. Promptly upon receiving the cup,
each recipient's face took on a stunned look. When it
came time for the pastor to receive, he discovered the
reason for the strange looks: The juice was prune juice!
One parishioner stated, "Perhaps this is a divine commen-
tary on our spirituality. . .we need a little loosening up!"

In line to receive communion one Sunday, the cell phone
of one woman went off just as the priest was giving her
a wafer. The woman turned beet red, stammered

JONATHAN KETCHUM'S CANNONBALL INTO THE BAPTISTRY WILL LONG BE REMEMBERED AT FEENEY ROAD BAPTIST CHURCH.

an apology, and attempted to get her phone shut off. Without skipping a beat, the priest said, "Tell them we don't do takeout."

A young son of a Baptist minister was in church one morning when he first observed baptism by immersion. His interest piqued, the next morning he attempted to baptize his three cats in the bathtub. The first kitten bore it very well, and so did the young cat, but the old family cat rebelled. It fought with him, scratched him, and then escaped. With considerable effort he caught it again and proceeded with the ceremony. But she acted worse than ever, clawed at him, spit, and scratched his hands and face. Finally, after hardly even a sprinkle, he dropped her on the floor in disgust and said: "Fine, be an atheist."

After coming out of the water, a new member exclaimed, "Good grief, Preacher, I forgot to take my wallet out of my pocket. It's dripping wet."

"Hallelujah," rejoiced the preacher, "we could stand a few more baptized wallets."

After a hearty rainstorm filled all the potholes in the streets and alleys, a young mother watched her two little boys playing in the puddle through her kitchen window.

The older of the two, a five-year-old lad, grabbed his brother by the back of his head and shoved his face into

A mother decided it was time that her three sons get baptized. On the designated Sunday morning as they were on their way to church, the mother noticed that her nine-year-old seemed to be a bit preoccupied.

When she asked him what the problem was, he said, "Mom, I want to go first."

"Why do you want to go first?" she asked.

"Because," he began and then paused for a few seconds, "I really don't want to be baptized in water that has all of my brothers' sins floating around in it."

the water hole. As the boy recovered and stood laughing and dripping, the mother ran to the yard in a panic.

"What are you doing to your little brother?" she exclaimed as she pulled her younger child close.

"We were just playing church, Mommy," he said. "And I was just baptizing him. . .in the name of the Father, the Son, and in. . .the hole-he-goes."

There was an old sinner who would get religion every time special meetings were held. Once the services ended he would go back to his old ways until the next revival meeting. After about six times at the baptizing hole, the preacher put him under and brought him back up and commented, "You've been dunked so many times that even the fish know you by your first name."

One young lad was known to be a nice boy, but he was not too bright. He just moved about life at his own pace, following his mama wherever she went. One year the boy's mother trusted Jesus and wanted to be baptized. As the baptismal service began, the congregation gathered at the river and began singing "Shall We Gather at the River" and "Are You Washed in the Blood." One by one the converts entered the water and were baptized. Soon it was the mother's turn. She entered the river, but right behind her was her son. When she came up and began to make her way to the riverbank, her son was right behind her. The preacher, thinking her son was next, grabbed him and began to baptize him with the boy

"AND THAT'S UNLEAVENED BREAD, FRED, NOT UNLEADED."

kicking and fighting the whole time. Finally the whole ordeal ended, and the boy made his way back to the bank. He shook the water off of himself and began to examine the contents of his pockets.

"Well, boys," he said to the crowd, "looks like I lost fifteen cents in the round."

A father took his three young children, including his five-year-old daughter, to church.

As usual, he sat in the front row so that the children could properly observe the service. During this particular service, the minister was performing the baptism of a tiny infant. The little five-year-old girl was mesmerized, as she observed the ceremony. With a quizzical look on her face, the little girl turned to her father and asked, "Daddy, why is he brainwashing that baby?"

✚ ✚ ✚

At the racetrack a man couldn't believe what he saw. There, in one of the stalls, a priest appeared to be blessing a horse before a race. Curious, the man paid special attention to the horse and was astounded when he discovered the horse came in first. After the race, the man noticed the priest doing the same thing again to another horse. . .and once again, the horse came in first in its race.

The man hurried to his bank and quickly emptied his savings account and then rushed back to the track. When he found the priest in the stall with another horse, he quickly placed all his money on that horse—and then eagerly waited for the race to begin. To his dismay, this horse didn't come in first, second, or third. . .in fact, the horse didn't even finish the race.

When the man questioned the priest about what happened, the priest shook his head. "That's the trouble with you Protestants," the priest said. "You can't tell the difference between a blessing and last rites!"

✚ ✚ ✚

The children were learning about communion during Sunday school. The teacher told them: "The Bible talks of Holy Communion being a 'joyful feast.' What does that mean? Well, *joyful* means happy, right? And a *feast* is a meal. So a 'joyful feast' is truly just a happy meal!"

The teacher paused and asked, "What are three things we need for a happy meal?"

A little boy put up his hand and said, "Hamburger, fries, and a regular soft drink!"

The Spiritual Gifts

ALTAR EGO by Len Jones

"I was just fine until you stood up in service and testified that golf was one of your spiritual gifts."

After a woman sang a "less than blessed" solo during the Lenten service, one man whispered to his wife, "She must have given up melody for Lent!"

At a Sunday service the violin solo was performed by a well-dressed college student. After church the performer's brother jabbed him in the ribs and said, "How come you look so sharp yet play so flat?"

The sound technicians always forgot to turn off the pastor's lapel microphone during the singing. "He has a great ear for music," one member of the congregation said to his wife.

"Too bad he doesn't have the voice for it!" his wife replied.

The church organist was known for hitting a few wrong keys each Sunday. One week, though, after practicing for several days, she played every song perfectly. "Wow, she played like she's never played before!" a surprised woman said to her husband.

"Yeah," he replied. "In tune!"

The pastor's desk was in need of repair so he went out and bought a new one. The trouble was that some assembly was required. After two hours of trying to put it together, the frazzled pastor walked out to where his secretary was working. "Being handy is *not* one of my spiritual gifts!" he exclaimed. "The store manager told me that a child can assemble this. So, could you run out and borrow a child?"

Getting to know a new couple at church, the pastor was asking about their spiritual gifts. "Can either of you teach or sing or play an instrument?"

"My wife is a great teacher," the man replied. "But the last time she sang at home, all of the dogs in the neighborhood came over to join her!"

A pastor who had been blessed with the gift of humor along with the gift of teaching began his salvation message as follows: "This is a dangerous world we live in. Yes. . .very few get out alive!"

One man in the choir could not sing a note in tune if his life depended on it. Several people hinted to him that he would make an excellent usher, but he continued to go to choir practice. The choir director and some members of the choir became desperate and pleaded with the pastor.

"You've got to get that man out of the choir," they begged. "If you don't, our Christmas cantata will be ruined and the other choir members will quit. Please do something!"

So the pastor went to the man and suggested, "Perhaps you should leave the choir."

"Why should I quit the choir?" he asked.

"Well, I hate to say this because I have no ear for music, but five or six people have told me that you can't sing."

"That's nothing." The man snorted. "Twenty-five people have told me that you can't preach!"

How many singers does it take to change a light bulb?

Only one, but she'll need six weeks' preparation and will get upset if you don't spell her name correctly in the bulletin.

Every morning an elderly woman would step out on her porch, raise her arms to heaven, and shout, "Praise God!"

An atheist happened to buy the house next door to her, and over the months he became very irritated with the spiritual woman. After six months of hearing her shout "Praise God" each morning, he went outside on his porch and yelled, "There is no God!"

The godly woman wasn't put off in the least. She continued to praise God every day. One cold winter morning the atheist heard the woman shout a different message.

"Help me, Lord," the woman prayed. "It's very cold and I am out of food and money."

When the woman went outside the next morning, there was enough food on the porch to last her a month.

"Praise God!" she shouted.

The atheist stepped out from the bushes and said, "There is no God! I bought all of those groceries!"

The woman raised her arms to the sky and said, "Praise God! You sent me groceries and made the devil pay for them!"

Why are an organist's fingers like lightning?

Because they seldom strike the same place twice.

How many choir directors does it take to change a light bulb?

Nobody knows. Nobody ever watches the choir director.

You should join the church choir:

if you want to see if the pastor has notes or has memorized his sermon.

if you want to make sure you always have a seat in an overcrowded church.

because the offering plate is never passed in the choir loft.

because choir robes are flattering for every body type.

because you can always watch the big clock at the back

"I'm here to tune your piano," said a man to the church pianist.

"But I never called you," the pianist replied in confusion.

"No, but quite a few church members did!" replied the man.

of the church without turning around.

so you can see anyone who falls asleep during the service—and then give them a hard time about it after church.

A woman loved to sing and decided to try out for the church choir. Every night she would practice and as soon as she began singing, the family dog began to howl loudly.

After a few nights of this, her husband had had enough.

"For goodness' sake, dear!" her husband shouted. "Can you please sing something the dog doesn't know?"

"I once sang for the king of Spain," announced an elderly woman during choir practice.

"You're kidding!" said the woman sitting next to her.

"Well, that's what he told me. He said that if I were a singer, then he was the king of Spain!"

A junior-high boy with a prematurely deep voice had been pressed into service in the church choir. Unfortunately, he lacked all knowledge of music.

"In the basic choir," the director explained, "there are two male vocal parts. One is the tenor. Do you know the other?"

"Well, uh," the boy stammered, "the elevener?"

Tithes and Offerings

ALTAR EGO by Len Jones

"I THINK GOD KNOWS HOW YOU REALLY FEEL, DON'T YOU?"

A little boy was sitting through the church service for the first time. As the usher passed an offering plate down his pew, the boy said, "Daddy, don't pay for me—I'm under five."

Shortly before morning worship, a minister was preoccupied with thoughts of how he could ask the congregation for more money for church repairs. He was even more troubled when he learned the regular organist was sick. When the last-minute substitute asked what to play, the pastor replied with a sigh, "Whatever you think best."

Opening the service with announcements, the pastor said, "Brothers and sisters, we are in great difficulty. The roof repairs have cost twice as much as we expected and we need another $4,000. Anyone who can pledge a hundred dollars or more, please stand up."

At that moment, the organist began playing "The Star-Spangled Banner."

When two successful businessmen went sailing, a freak storm wrecked their boat and left them marooned on a deserted island. By the third day, one of the men was pacing constantly. The other reclined peacefully on the sand.

"Aren't you afraid we're going to die?" the first man wailed.

"Not at all," his friend replied. "I make almost a hundred thousand dollars a week, and I tithe faithfully to my church. My pastor will find me."

Inside a bank vault, the various denominations of money began to discuss the places they'd been. The hundred-dollar bills told of visiting Tokyo, Paris, and Rio. The twenties said they'd spent time in Las Vegas and Atlantic City. The ones, meanwhile, said they'd been traveling from church to church to church.

In a small church, the pastor waited for the offering to be taken. When the plate came back with even less money than usual, he began his prayer, "Well, Lord, we thank You for the safe return of the plate."

A preacher announced to his congregation: "I have good news and bad news. The good news is: we have enough money to pay for our new building program. The bad news is: it's still out there in your pockets."

A recent seminary graduate thought that before he took on a congregation, he needed more experience about why people are fearful and tempted in certain circumstances. He decided that the best way to do this would be to enroll in the police academy. One of the questions on his certification exam was: "In an emergency, how would you quickly and wisely disperse a frantic crowd?"

His answer: "Pass an offering plate."

NOW BROTHER HIGGENBOTHAM WILL PRESENT OUR
FINANCIAL REPORT.

"We welcome all denominations here," said the pastor before praying for the offering. "Especially tens and twenties!"

A pastor made an announcement as the ushers carried offering plates to the front of the sanctuary: "I would like to remind you that what you are about to give is tax deductible, cannot be taken with you, and the Bible says is a root of all evil."

"Were you a good girl at church today?" a grandmother asked her young relative.

"Oh yes," the girl replied. "When a nice man offered me a whole plate of money, I said, 'No, thank you.' "

The Sunday school teacher carefully explained why it's important for everyone to put their "tithes and offerings" in the plate every Sunday. At offering time, following his teacher's instructions, one seven-year-old boy removed his clip-on tie and placed it in the plate.

Heard the song by Ray Stevens? "If Ten Percent Is Good Enough for Jesus (It Ought to Be Enough for Uncle Sam)."

✝ ✝ ✝

A young boy was invited to church by one of his friends. On the way out the door, his mother handed him two dollars.

"One for you, and one for God," his mother said.

As the boy walked along with his friends, the wind blew his dollars right out of his hand and onto the street. One of them went right down into the sewer.

"Uh-oh!" the boy said. "There goes God's dollar!"

Buildings and Grounds

ALTAR EGO by Len Jones

"THE CHURCH BOARD WOULD LIKE TO REPORT THAT WE ARE STILL JUST A BIT SHORT OF OUR FUND RAISING GOAL FOR NEW SANCTUARY LIGHTING."

One church installed sanitary hot air hand dryers in the restrooms but after two weeks they were removed even though they worked just fine. When asked why the dryers had been removed, the pastor said that he'd gone in the restroom and discovered a sign that read, FOR A SAMPLE OF THIS WEEK'S SERMON, PUSH THE BUTTON.

A man who was filling out an application for employment came to the question "What is your church preference?"

The man, not being a person of extraordinary intelligence or deep religious conviction, thought about the question for some time because he really needed the job. Wanting to impress the employer, he answered confidently, "I prefer a red brick church."

The crumbling old church desperately needed remodeling, so the preacher made an impassioned appeal, obviously directed at the wealthiest man in town. At the end of the message, the rich man stood up and announced, "Pastor, I will contribute $1,000."

Just then, a chunk of plaster fell from the ceiling and struck the rich man on the shoulder. He promptly stood again and shouted, "Pastor, I will increase my donation to $5,000." Before he could sit back down, plaster fell on him again, and again he virtually screamed, "Pastor, I will double my last pledge."

As he sat down, a larger chunk of plaster fell, hitting him on the head. He stood once more and hollered, "Pastor, I will give $20,000!"

At this a deacon shouted, "Hit him again, Lord! Hit him again!"

During an ecumenical assembly, a secretary rushed in shouting, "The building is on fire!"

The Methodists prayed in a corner.

The Baptists wondered where they could find water.

The Quakers quietly praised God for the blessings that fire brings.

The Lutherans posted a notice on the door announcing the fire was evil.

The Roman Catholics passed the plate to cover the cost of the damage.

The Jews posted symbols on the door in hopes the fire would pass.

The Congregationalists shouted, "Every man for himself!"

The Fundamentalists proclaimed, "It's the vengeance of God!"

The Episcopalians formed a procession and protested.

The Christian Scientists denied that there was a fire.

The Presbyterians appointed a chairperson to form a committee to look into the matter and submit a written report.

The secretary grabbed the fire extinguisher and put the fire out.

When a deacon went to New York for a vacation, his pastor requested that he order a sign that would be put over the church door at Christmas. On the last day of his vacation the deacon finally remembered that he needed to order the sign but he couldn't remember the specifics of the request so he sent a wire to the pastor. The receptionist at the telegraph office nearly collapsed when the pastor's response came in: "Unto us a child is born. Eight feet long, three feet wide."

After calling around to various professional painters in the area, a church selected one to paint the exterior of the building. Because this particular painter's bid was about half of what his competitor's had been, it was an easy decision to give him the job.

On the morning the job began, the painter realized that he had underbid the job by 50 percent! Not wanting to request the additional funds, he decided to thin out the paint with water so he would be able to complete the job for the price quoted.

One week later, he received a call from the pastor, who was wondering why after the first rain half of the paint had washed off the church. The painter returned and looked at the building and then went inside to pray about the situation, knowing that his reputation was on the line. "What can I possibly do, Lord?" prayed the discouraged painter.

Suddenly, God, in a loud voice from the altar, replied, "Repaint, and thin no more!"

There was an inscription in stone over the great front doors of an old church building that was being restored. It said, This is the Gate of Heaven.

Just below the inscription someone had placed a small cardboard sign which read: PLEASE USE OTHER ENTRANCE.

A visitor who had taken her baby to the restroom for a diaper change noticed a sign over the changing station. It read: WE SHALL NOT ALL SLEEP BUT WE SHALL BE CHANGED.

A minister in a new parish was presenting the children's message. Because the sanctuary in the church had some magnificent stained glass windows, with each depicting a story from the Bible, the minister's message centered on how each of us is called to help make up the whole picture of life. Like the pictures in the windows, it takes many little panels of glass to make the whole picture.

And then he said, "You see each one of you is a little pane." And then pointing to each child, "You're a little pane. And you're a little pane. And you're a little pane. And. . ."

It took a few moments before he realized why everyone was laughing so hard.

The minister of a small church knew that improvements were needed on the church building. He suggested purchasing a chandelier, but the church members voted it down.

"Why are you opposed to buying a chandelier?" the preacher questioned.

"First, no one can spell it," said the spokesperson. "Second, no one can play it. And finally, what we really need is more light."

A rich man went to his vicar and said, "I want you and your wife to take a three-month, all-expense-paid vacation to the Holy Land. When you return, I'll have a surprise for you." The vicar accepted the offer, and he and his wife went off to the Middle East.

Three months later, they returned home and were met by the wealthy parishioner, who told them that while they were gone, he had had a new church built. "It's the finest building money can buy, Vicar," said the man. "No expense was spared." And he was right. It was a fabulous construction both outside and in.

But there was one odd detail. There was only one pew, and it was at the very back. "A church with only one pew?" questioned the vicar.

"You just wait until Sunday," the rich man said.

When the time came for the Sunday service, the early arrivals entered the church, filed onto the one pew, and sat down. When the pew was full, a switch clicked silently, a circuit closed, the gears meshed, a belt moved, and automatically the rear pew began to move forward. When it reached the front of the church, it came to a stop. At the same time, another empty pew came up from below at the back and more people sat down. And so it continued, pews filling and moving forward until finally the church was full, from front to back.

"Wonderful!" said the vicar. "Marvelous!"

The service began and the vicar started to preach his sermon. He was so happy to be back and so thrilled with the new building that he lost track of time. He launched into his sermon and, when twelve o'clock came, he was still going strong with no end in sight. Suddenly a bell rang, and a trap door in the floor behind the pulpit dropped open.

"Wonderful!" said the congregation. "Marvelous!"

✛ ✛ ✛

Following the death of Quasimodo, the bishop of the Cathedral Church of Notre Dame sent word throughout the streets of Paris that a new bell ringer would need to be appointed. The bishop decided that he would himself conduct the interviews, and he went up into the belfry to interview the candidates. After observing several applicants demonstrate their skills, he decided to call it a day. At that moment an armless man approached him announcing that he was there to apply for the post.

The bishop was stunned and declared, "My son, you have no arms!"

"Just give me a chance," replied the man. He then proceeded to strike the bells with his face, producing the most beautiful melody ever heard on the carillon. The bishop was astonished and instantly believed this man was indeed a suitable replacement for Quasimodo. But in rushing forward to strike a bell, the armless man tripped, and plunged headlong out of the belfry to his death in the street below. The bishop immediately rushed to his side. When he reached the street, a crowd had gathered around the fallen figure, drawn by the beauty of the music they had heard but a moment before. As they parted in silence to allow the bishop through, one of the number asked quietly, "Bishop, who was this man?"

"I don't know his name," replied the bishop sadly, "but his face rings a bell."

The following day, despite the sadness that weighed heavily on his heart, the bishop continued his interviews for a bell ringer for Notre Dame. The first man to approach addressed him, "Your Grace, I am the brother of the poor man who fell to his death from this belfry yesterday. I pray that you will allow me to replace him." The bishop, feeling obligated, agreed to an audition, but as the man reached to strike the first bell, he groaned, clutched at his chest, collapsed, and died on the spot. Two monks, hearing the cries of grief from the bishop at the tragedy, rushed up the stairs. "What has happened? Who is this man?" they cried.

"I don't know his name," exclaimed the distraught bishop, "but he's a dead ringer for his brother."

A minister was walking to church one morning when he passed one of his members working in his garden. "The bells are calling you to church this fine morning," admonished the minister.

"What did you say?" asked the member.

"Can't you hear those bells calling you to church?"

"I'm afraid you'll have to speak a little louder!" said the member.

"CAN'T YOU HEAR THOSE BELLS CALLING YOU TO CHURCH?!" shouted the minister.

"I'm sorry," said the member, "I can't hear you because of those noisy BELLS!"

A preacher was explaining to his congregation how the new sound system had come to be. "The microphone and wiring were paid for by the church," he said. "And the loudspeaker was donated by Mr. Thomas in memory of his wife."

✚ ✚ ✚

In a cathedral that is being constructed, the workers have put together a "cage elevator" inside so they can get material to the upper floors. A characteristic of these cage elevators is that the gate must be closed manually for them to be "called" to another floor.

One day one of the workers named Peter took the elevator to the top floor, and it was soon needed on the first floor by the sexton. Unfortunately, Peter accidentally left the door open. After the sexton rang for the elevator a couple times with no results, he yelled up for the worker to send the lift back down. Visitors to the cathedral were treated to this sight: The sexton of the cathedral, head tipped up, yelling up to the heavens:

"Peter! CLOSE THE GATES!"

A monastery in Europe is perched high on a cliff several hundred feet in the air. Though it is a treacherous journey to reach it, many tourists are drawn to its beauty and mystery.

The only way to reach the monastery is to step into a basket which is then pulled to the top by several monks pulling and tugging with all their might.

Obviously the ride up the steep cliff in that basket is terrifying. One tourist got exceedingly nervous about halfway up as he noticed that the rope by which he was suspended was weak and beginning to unravel.

With a trembling voice he asked the monk who was riding with him in the basket how often they changed the rope. The monk thought for a moment and answered brusquely, "Whenever it breaks."

✛ ✛ ✛

An elderly priest, speaking to a younger priest, said, "It was a good idea to replace the first four pews with plush bucket theater seats. It has worked like a charm. The front of the church always fills first now."

The young priest nodded, and the old priest continued, "And you gave me some good ideas for bringing back the young people. Now our services are consistently packed to the balcony."

"Thank you, Father," answered the young priest, beaming that the older man appreciated his suggestions.

"All of these ideas have been well and good," said the elderly priest, "but I'm afraid you've gone too far with the drive-through confessional."

"But, Father," protested the young priest, "my confessions and the donations have nearly doubled since I began that!"

"Yes," replied the elderly priest, "and I appreciate that. But the flashing neon sign on the church roof, TOOT 'N' TELL OR GO TO HELL, has to go!"

Some friars were behind on their belfry payments, so they opened up a small florist shop to raise the funds.

Since everyone liked to buy flowers from the men of God, the florist across town began to lose business. Thinking this was unfair, he asked the priests to close down, but they would not. He went back and begged them to close. Still they refused. Then the rival florist, becoming desperate, hired the roughest and most vicious thug in town, a man named Hugh, to "persuade" them to close.

The thug beat up the friars and trashed their store,

saying he'd be back if they didn't close up shop.
Terrified, they did so.

And all this goes to prove that Hugh, and Hugh alone,
can prevent florist friars.

The new pastor of a small church dropped into a Sunday
school class and began asking a few questions.

"Who knocked down the walls of Jericho?" he
wanted to know.

"It wasn't me, Reverend!" one little boy declared.

Turning to the teacher, the pastor exclaimed, "Is this
a sample of the kind of class you maintain?"

"Now, Reverend," the teacher responded, "he's a
good boy and doesn't tell lies. If he said he didn't do it, I
believe him."

Thoroughly annoyed, the pastor went to the church's
deacon board. After due consideration, the board sent
the following message to the minister: "We see no point
in making an issue of this incident. The church should
pay for the damages to Jericho's wall and charge it off to
vandalism."

A preacher went to his church office on Monday
morning and found a dead mule in the churchyard. He
called the police, but because there did not appear to
be any foul play, the police told the preacher to call the
health department.

The health department said since there was
no health threat that he should call the sanitation
department.

The sanitation manager said the preacher would have to get authorization from the mayor before the sanitation department could pick up the mule.

Now the preacher knew the mayor and was not too eager to call him. The mayor had a bad temper and was generally hard to deal with, but the preacher called him anyway.

The mayor, true to form, began to grumble. Ranting and raving, he finally challenged the pastor, "Why did you call me anyway? Isn't it your job to bury the dead?"

The preacher paused for a brief prayer and asked the Lord to direct his response. He was led to say, "Yes, Mayor, it is my job to bury the dead, but I always like to notify the next of kin first!"

A local church built a new sanctuary. They wanted to move their very fine old pipe organ from the old building to the new sanctuary. It was a delicate task that was completed successfully. The local newspaper heralded, SAINT PAUL COMPLETES ORGAN TRANSPLANT.

The church custodian prided herself on keeping the building spotless. However, she began to notice several brown bags under the pews each week. Usually she picked them up and threw them away, but curiosity got the best of her and she decided to check them out. Upon opening a couple she went straight to the pastor's office.

"Pastor," she began. "You might want to consider cutting the length of your sermons. People are starting to bring their lunches."

"I FEEL TERRIBLE. I TOLD ARNOLD THAT GOING TO CHURCH ONCE WOULDN'T HURT HIM. . .THEN THAT CHANDELIER FELL ON HIM!"

A pastor wanted to have a hole cut into the outside wall of his office so that an air conditioner could be installed. He called a reputable construction company and they agreed to come. However, several weeks passed, and no one showed up. Soon he got a bill for the job. He called the company to protest. The voice on the other end said, "Hold just a moment please." Soon the receptionist came back on the line. "In the spirit of ecumenism, we cut the hole in the Catholic church."

A professional organist was hired to play for a wedding. Not being familiar with the church's organ, she went to the sanctuary to practice. Wondering about a small keyboard that pulled out from under the two regular keyboards, she played a few measures of a children's song but heard nothing. Then she played a few more notes, but still no organ music.

Just then a deacon came running into the church, exclaiming, "Who's playing 'Mary Had a Little Lamb' on the steeple bells?"

The newly appointed priest was being briefed by the housekeeper on problems in the rectory that needed immediate attention. "Your roof leaks, Father," she said. "Your water pressure is bad and your furnace is not working."

"You've been the housekeeper here five years, and I've only been here a few days. You might as well say 'our roof and our furnace,' " the pastor cajoled.

Several weeks later, when the pastor was meeting with the bishop and several other priests, the housekeeper burst into the office, terribly shaken. "Father, Father," she blurted, "there's a mouse in our room and it's under our bed!"

The 104-year-old building that had served as the priory and primary student residence of the small Catholic university was about to be demolished. As the wrecker's ball began to strike, agitation and sadness were displayed on the face of one of the older monks whose order had founded the college. "This must be difficult to watch, Father," someone said. "The memories of all the students and monks who lived and worked there must be rushing back to you. I can't imagine how hard this must be for you."

"It's worse than that," the monk replied. "I think I left my Palm Pilot in there."

A pastor was negotiating with a contractor for repairs to his roof. "Go easy on me," the minister pleaded. "I'm just a poor preacher."

"I know," the tradesperson replied. "I heard you speak last Sunday."

People walking into a church hall were surprised by a sign placed there by the janitor, who had just mopped the tile floor: PLEASE DO NOT WALK ON THE WATER.

Around Town

"THIS OUGHT' A BRING THOSE STRAYS IN POD'NAH!"

A pastor's son who had just gotten his driving permit asked his dad if they could discuss the use of the car. The pastor said to his son, "I'll make a deal with you. You bring your grades up, study your Bible regularly, and get your hair cut, and we'll talk about it."

A month later, the boy came back and again asked to discuss the use of the family car. The pastor replied, "Son, I've been real proud of you. You've brought your grades up and you've studied your Bible diligently. But you never got your hair cut."

"You know, Dad, I've been thinking about that," the young man replied. "Samson had long hair, Moses and Noah probably had long hair. All the pictures of Jesus show Him with long hair. . . ."

"Yes," the pastor interrupted, "and they walked everywhere they went!"

A man was hiking on a nature trail when a bear appeared. The bear gave chase, so the man clambered up the nearest tree. But as he was climbing, he slipped and fell at the feet of the beast.

"Lord, please let this be a Christian bear." The man gasped.

And the bear said, "Heavenly Father, I thank You for this food."

A man decided to go ice fishing. Walking onto the frozen surface, he pitched his tent, propped up his fishing rod, and started to pick at the ice. Suddenly, a booming voice rang out: "THERE ARE NO FISH UNDER THE ICE!"

Startled, the man stopped and looked around. Seeing no one, he shrugged his shoulder and started to pick at the ice again. The voice returned: "THERE ARE NO FISH UNDER THE ICE!"

Feeling a bit spooked, the man looked up and said, "God, is that You?"

"NO," the voice responded. "I'M THE MANAGER OF THIS RINK, TALKING TO YOU ON THE PUBLIC ADDRESS SYSTEM!"

The big-city denominational office had sent a female pastor to serve in an old country church—and the local elders were having a hard time accepting the new minister. But they wanted to be gracious, so the board invited the pastor to join them on a fishing trip.

Once at the lake, the group got into a boat and motored out some fifty yards from shore when the pastor announced, apologetically, "I'm so sorry—I've forgotten my fishing rod."

So she stepped out of the boat, walked across the water to the bank, and picked up her equipment, and walked on the water back to the boat.

"Just like a woman," one of the elders muttered. "Always forgetting something!"

A noted evangelist arrived in a large city to hold a crusade. At a kick-off banquet his first night in town, he noticed some reporters in the audience.

The evangelist told the reporters that he'd be sharing some stories at the dinner that he planned to tell in his sermons the coming week. So as not to ruin the effect of the stories, he asked the reporters to omit them from their articles the next day.

In the following day's paper, a cub reporter described the dinner, concluding with this line: "The evangelist also told a number of stories that cannot be printed."

✛ ✛ ✛

A church member went to the butcher's shop one afternoon to pick up some salmon.

"I want four big ones," the man said. "Just toss them to me."

The butcher looked strangely at the man. "Can't I just wrap them up for you?"

"No," the customer replied. "If anyone from church asks me if I caught any fish today, I can truthfully tell them, 'Yes, I caught four big ones!' "

✛ ✛ ✛

Between services, a church member noticed a passing driver flick a cigarette out of his window into some shrubbery on the church property. The bush smoldered then burst into flame.

The church member ran to the office, phoned the fire department, explained the situation, and asked for help.

"You mean to tell me there's a burning bush on the church lawn," the dispatcher replied, "and you want us to put it out?"

A Jewish rabbi and a Catholic priest met at the town's annual carnival. They had been friends for a long time and launched into their usual banter.

"This baked ham is so delicious!" the priest teased. "You really ought to try it. I know it's against your religion, but I can't understand why such a wonderful food should be forbidden. You don't know what you're missing! Tell me, friend, when are you going to give in and try it?"

The rabbi looked at the priest and responded, "At your wedding, of course!"

A collector of rare books ran into an acquaintance who told him he had just thrown away an old Bible that he found in a dusty old box. He happened to mention that "Guten-somebody-or-other" had printed it.

"Not Gutenberg?" gasped the collector.

"Yes, I think that was it."

"Are you crazy? You've thrown away one of the first books ever printed. A copy recently sold at auction for half a million dollars!"

"Oh, I don't think this book would have been worth a whole lot," replied the man. "Some guy named Martin Luther scribbled all over the margins."

"Why don't you come to our church?" a little boy asked his best friend.

"Because my family belongs to another abomination," he replied.

A man went to the pastor for counseling. He was overwhelmed with life.

"God will never give you more than you can handle," the pastor counseled.

"Well, then, I wish He didn't trust me so much!" replied the man.

After twenty years of shaving himself every morning, a man in a small southern town decided he had been doing that long enough. He told his wife that from then on he'd let the local barber shave him each day.

The man went to the barber shop which was owned by the pastor of the local Baptist church. The barber's wife, whose name was Grace, shaved him and sprayed him with lilac water. "That will be twenty dollars," she said. The man thought the price was a bit high and wondered how he'd continue to foot such a bill, but he paid for the service and went off to work.

The next morning, the man looked in the mirror and saw that his face was as smooth as it had been when he left the barber shop the day before. *Not bad*, he thought. *At least I don't need to get a shave every day.* The next morning, the man's face was still smooth. Two weeks later, the man was still unable to find any trace of whiskers on his face. He couldn't understand it, so he returned to the barber shop.

"I thought twenty dollars was high for a shave," he told the barber's wife, "but you must have done a great job. It's been two weeks and my whiskers still haven't started growing back."

The woman's face showed no surprise. "Well, of

course," she said. "You were shaved by Grace. Once shaved, always shaved."

Retirees on a plane headed for Florida were gripped with fear when the pilot announced, "Two of our engines are on fire. We are flying through a heavy fog and have virtually zero visibility."

The passengers were numb with fear, except for one, a semiretired minister. "Now, now, keep calm, folks," he said. "Let's all bow our heads and pray."

Immediately, the group bowed their heads to pray, except one fellow near the back.

"Why aren't you bowing your head to pray?" the minister asked.

"I don't know much about prayer," the man replied.

"Well, at least try to do something religious," the minister begged.

The man then grabbed a hat and started passing it.

After many years apart, two high school friends reunited and discussed their careers. One said he had attended college and worked hard to become a success but had recently fallen on hard times. The other admitted he'd dropped out of college his freshman year and was pretty lazy.

The first one asked, "So what have you been doing all these years?"

"Well," the lazy friend answered, "one day I opened my Bible at random, closed my eyes, and dropped my finger on a word. The word was *oil*, so I invested the little money I had in oil and did very well. Later, I opened my Bible again, closed my eyes, and dropped my finger on the word *gold*. So I invested my oil profits in gold, and those mines really produced. Now I'm one of the richest men in America!"

The college-educated friend was so impressed that he rushed back to his hotel, grabbed a Gideon Bible, closed his eyes, and dropped his finger on a page. When he opened his eyes, he was horrified to find the words, *Chapter Eleven*.

A college freshman was sitting on a campus bench holding an open Bible and shouting, "Hallelujah! God is great!"

Before long, a skeptical professor happened by. Hearing the young man's praises, he asked what he was reading.

"The book of Exodus," the freshman replied. "Did you know what God is able to do? I just read that He parted the Red Sea and led the whole nation of Israel right through the middle."

The professor chuckled, sat down next to the young man, and decided to share the latest theories on the Bible account. "That can all be very easily explained," the professor said. "Modern scholarship has shown that the Red Sea in that area was only ten inches deep at that time. It would have been no problem for the Israelites simply to wade across."

The young man was quiet for a moment, his gaze slowly moving from the professor back to the open Bible in his lap. The skeptic, satisfied that he had set the young man straight, got up to leave.

But before the professor had taken two steps, the

young man began to shout again, "Hallelujah! God is great!"

At a loss for words, the professor asked, "What. . . why. . .?"

"God is greater than I thought!" the freshman gushed. "Not only did He lead the whole nation of Israel through the Red Sea, He drowned the whole Egyptian army in ten inches of water!"

A man dashed into a restaurant to get out of the pouring rain.

"Looks like the great flood out there!" the man exclaimed.

"The what?" asked the waitress.

"You know. . .Noah and the great flood?" said the man.

"Sorry, I don't know what you mean," replied the waitress. "I haven't watched TV in four days!"

A man was driving to work when a truck ran a stop sign, hit his car broadside, and knocked him cold. Passersby pulled him from the wreck and gave him CPR. He began to thrash terribly and had to be tranquilized by the medics.

Later, when he was calm, they asked him why he struggled so. He said, "I remember the impact, then nothing. I woke up on a concrete slab in front of a huge flashing SHELL sign. . .only somebody was standing in front of the S!"

"I DON'T LIKE TO SPREAD GOSSIP, PASTOR, BUT WHAT ELSE CAN YOU DO WITH IT?"

A group of university scientists approached a local pastor to tell him that God was no longer needed. "We've created spaceships, supercomputers, almost life itself," the scientists said. "Human knowledge has advanced to the point that God Himself is obsolete."

The pastor listened politely, then said, "I'd like some proof of that. Can you create a human being, like God did with Adam?"

"Sure!" the scientists replied. They invited the pastor to their labs.

At the university, one group of scientists invited the pastor to join them as they prepared an operating table for the big moment. Soon, the other group appeared, carrying buckets of dirt from which to make a man.

"Hey, wait a minute," the pastor said. "That's God's dirt. . .go make your own!"

The pastor, a well-known foe of sex and violence on television, had been invited to participate in a community discussion on entertainment. A young man in the audience, hoping to show the pastor up, asked him a question: "Pastor, why is television known as a 'medium'?"

"That's because it's neither rare nor well done," the pastor replied.

A sixth-grade teacher in the public school called a student to her desk after class. "Why did you say in your essay that you're Jewish? I know your father is a pastor in town."

"That's because I can't spell *Presbyterian*!" the boy answered.

Before listening to her young patients' heartbeats, a pediatric nurse at the hospital would often fit the stethoscope over their ears and allow them to listen first.

One four-year-old boy was awed by the sound. The nurse asked him, "What do you suppose that is?"

The child, a regular at Sunday school, answered, "Is that Jesus knocking?"

A young security guard was posted to the overnight shift outside a bank. Try as he might, he couldn't stay awake for the entire eight hours. His head slumped to his chest and he fell fast asleep.

Around 4:00 a.m., he awoke with a start to see his supervisor eyeing him suspiciously. Knowing the trouble he'd face for sleeping on the job, he lowered his head once more and intoned, "Ah-men."

A young mother and her five-year-old daughter were driving to a fast-food restaurant. On their way, two fire trucks and an ambulance raced past them.

As was her custom, the mother offered a prayer for

whoever was in trouble. Then she asked her daughter if she would like to pray, too.

"Dear Jesus," the little girl said, "please don't let that be an accident in front of the restaurant."

One Sunday morning, a motorcycle patrol officer pulled over a car for speeding. As the officer was preparing a ticket, several cars drove by with people honking and waving.

After the ninth such response, the officer asked the driver what was going on.

"I'm the pastor at the church just up the road," the man replied. "That's where I was headed when you stopped me. Those are members of my congregation who recognized me."

The officer smiled and tore up the ticket. "I think you've paid your debt to society," he said.

A kindergarten teacher gave her class a "show and tell" assignment, asking each student to bring in an object that represented their religion.

The first student stood in front of the class and said, "My name is Benjamin. I'm Jewish, and this is a Star of David."

Another student stood and said, "My name is Mary. I'm Catholic, and this is a rosary."

A third student walked to the front of the room. "My name is Tommy," he said. "I'm a Baptist, and this is a casserole."

✦ ✦ ✦

A volunteer youth leader took a group of teens on a hike. Hearing the sounds of baby birds, he fell back from the group to try to find the nest.

Unfortunately, the leader stepped over the edge of a cliff—but was able to grab a slender tree branch before falling all the way to the floor of the gorge. Unable to get back onto the ledge, the man prayed—and suddenly heard a voice from heaven. "I am the Lord. I can help you. Do you believe that?"

"Of course!" the man replied. "I trust you completely, Lord!"

"Then let go," God said. "I will take care of you."

The man hung in silence for a moment.

"Well," God said, "what do you say?"

"I say," the man replied, "is there anybody else up there?"

Working Together

ALTAR EGO™ by Len Jones

"CHEF SCHOOL OR NO CHEF SCHOOL. . . . I'VE TOLD YOU A HUNDRED TIMES. WE ARE SERVING COMMUNION NOT BRUNCH!"

Top Ten Things You Won't Hear in Church:

10. Forget the salary we voted on, let's pay our pastor so he can live like we do.
9. I was so captivated by your sermon, I didn't even notice you went forty-five minutes over time.
8. I would love to volunteer as the permanent teacher for the junior-high Sunday school class.
7. Pastor, we'd like to send you to a Bible conference in Hawaii.
6. I've decided to give the church an extra $600 a month that I used to put in savings!
5. Nothing makes me more excited than our annual stewardship drive!
4. Let's sit in the very front row today.
3. I find door-to-door evangelism much more enjoyable than golf.
2. I love it when we sing songs I've never heard before.
1. Since we're all here a bit early, why don't we go ahead and start?

A pastor was talking with a member of his church.

"You know," the pastor said, "I wish I had ten members just like you."

"Really?" the parishioner responded. "I'm a little surprised to hear you say that. I realize that I often complain about your preaching, hardly give anything in the offering, and haven't volunteered my time for any of our ministries. Why would you want ten people just like me?"

"Like I said," the pastor replied, "I wish I had ten members like you. The problem is, I have fifty!"

✝ ✝ ✝

A pastor had just returned from vacation with a new idea. The church he had attended had stopped in the middle of the song service to allow people in the congregation to welcome each other. Impressed, the pastor said he'd be implementing the concept in the next week's service.

One church member, enthusiastic at the idea, turned to shake the hand of an older woman behind him. She fixed the man with an icy stare and said, "That friendliness business doesn't start until next week!"

✝ ✝ ✝

When the grumpy church secretary planned a vacation, the pastor decided to call a temporary agency for help.

After the secretary returned she asked the pastor, "So how'd that hotshot temp work out?"

"Well," the pastor responded, "it was pretty rough. She couldn't type more than thirty words a minute and she kept pestering me with basic questions about the computer. She couldn't figure out how to replace the copy machine paper, and she had terrible phone manners. In fact, she spent much of her time on the phone gossiping."

"That's pretty much what I expected." The secretary sneered.

"Yeah," the pastor replied, "it was pretty much as though you'd never left."

A teenager was telling his pastor about their church's volunteer youth leader, who was refusing to allow the boy to join in any future camping trips.

"Why not?" the pastor asked. "What happened?"

"I think he's mad because I lost our compass when we waded through a creek," the boy replied.

"He's that mad," the pastor asked, "because a little compass got lost?"

"Well, it wasn't just the compass," the teen responded. "We all got lost."

"GOSH, HONEY, I'M SORRY. I DIDN'T THINK YOU WOULD MIND HAVING ONE MORE JOB AT THE CHURCH."

✛ ✛ ✛

In a small town, three churches decided to work together to improve the community. The three preachers decided to meet regularly to mow lawns, paint houses, and perform other outreach in the village.

On their first day, they spent several hours in the sun, preparing a garden for a homeless shelter. They really enjoyed getting to know each other, and when the work was done, they sat in the shade sipping lemonade.

"You know, guys," one said, "this has been great. I've needed this kind of fellowship—and after one day with you, I feel like I really know you. Can I make a confession and ask you to pray for me? I have a terrible problem with alcohol."

The others agreed that they would pray for their friend. Then the second pastor spoke up. "This has been a marvelous day. And I have a special need, too. I've been a secret gambler for years. I just can't give it up. Will you pray for me?"

The other two pastors agreed to pray, when the third one announced, "Well, since we're sharing our secret faults today, I should let you know that I have a problem with gossip."

Have you heard of the Tate family? They're very prominent in many churches.

There's old Dick Tate who wants to run everything. Ro Tate tries to change everything. Sister Agi Tate stirs up plenty of trouble, with help from her husband, Irri Tate. When a new project is suggested, Hesi Tate and his wife, Vege Tate, always want to wait until next year. Then there's Imi Tate, who wants the church to be like all the others. Devas Tate always provides the voice of doom, while Poten Tate wants to be important.

Not every Tate is trouble, though. Cousins Cogi Tate and Medi Tate are the thoughtful types. Brother Facili Tate is quite helpful, and Miss Felici Tate is delightful. Just watch out for Ampu Tate.

Old-Time Church

"HOLD ON THERE, PREACHER. WE DON'T USE THOSE NEWFANGLED BIBLES HERE. . .WE BELIEVE IF THE KING JAMES WAS GOOD ENOUGH FOR PAUL, IT'S GOOD ENOUGH FOR US."

An old-time circuit-riding preacher found himself in need of money and decided to sell his horse and buggy. The local blacksmith was interested, and as they completed the deal, the pastor mentioned, "This is not an ordinary horse."

"What do you mean?" the blacksmith asked.

The preacher explained. "Since this horse has been owned and driven by a man of the cloth all his life, he does not respond to the commands of *whoa* or *giddy-up*. When you want this horse to stop you must say *Amen*. When you want him to go you must say *Praise the Lord!*

Later that day, the blacksmith took the horse out for a ride. Trotting down the road, the horse was startled by a snake and bolted. Soon it was careening full-speed toward a cliff.

Panicky, the blacksmith shouted "Whoa!" over and over until he remembered the preacher's instructions. A loud "Amen!" brought the horse to a stop at the edge of the cliff.

Relieved, the blacksmith wiped his brow and exclaimed, "Praise the Lord!"

An old-time pastor was riding furiously down the road, hurrying to get to church on time. Suddenly, his horse stumbled and threw him to the ground.

Lying in the dirt, his body wracked with pain, the pastor called out, "All you angels in heaven, help me get up on my horse!"

With extraordinary strength, he leaped onto the horse's back—and fell off the other side.

From the ground again, he called out, "All right, just half of you angels this time!"

On his way to church, a farm boy accidentally tipped over his wagon. A neighboring farmer, also on his way to church, heard the commotion and pulled up nearby.

"Hey, hop in with us," the neighbor said. "I'll help you get the wagon up after church."

"That's mighty nice of you," the boy answered, "but I don't think Pa would like me to."

"Come on," the Good Samaritan insisted. "If you don't hurry, we'll be late!"

"Well, okay," the boy finally agreed. "But Pa won't like it."

After church, the boy thanked his neighbor for the help. "I'm glad we got to church on time," he said, "but I know Pa is going to be real upset."

"Oh, he'll be fine," the neighbor said with a smile. "By the way, where is he?"

"Under the wagon."

✦ ✦ ✦

A guest preacher was traveling through New England and offered to preach at a friend's church. His friend declined the offer because his congregation had the habit of leaving before the service had ended. The guest preacher, however, saw this as a challenge. The next Sunday morning he announced to the assembly, "My hearers, I am going to speak to two sorts of folks today—saints and sinners! Sinners! I am going to give you your portion first, and would have you give good attention." When he had preached to them for a good amount of time, he paused and said, "There, sinners, I have done with you now; you may take your hats and go out of the meetinghouse as soon as you please." The church remained full to the close of the service.

Even without modern special effects, some old-time preachers still managed to be quite theatrical. One such preacher would hire a young boy to hide in the rafters with a caged dove. At the proper point in the message, the minister would raise his hands toward heaven and call, "Holy Ghost, come down!" The boy would release the dove, and it would fly down with great effect. But during one service the man called, "Holy Ghost, come down," and nothing happened. He tried again to no avail.

Movement was heard in the rafters and a little voice called out, "Preacher, a big old cat just ate the Holy Ghost. You want me to throw down the old cat?"

Many years ago the women of a particular community had the habit of wearing their hair in topknots. The preacher despised this style and delivered a highly animated message entitled "Topknot Come Down." At the end of the service a very angry parishioner with a very obvious topknot announced loudly that there was no such text in the scripture. The preacher, prepared for such an attack, opened to Matthew 24:17 and pointed to the words, "Let him which is on the housetop not come down to take anything out of the house."

A church in Louisiana wanted to purchase some land for their new church building and they hoped to finance this new facility with a government loan.

Their lawyer filled out all the necessary forms, including the abstract—tracing the title to the land back to 1803. The government reviewed his application and abstract and sent the following reply:

We received today your letter enclosing application for your client supported by abstract of title. We have observed, however, that you have not traced the title previous to 1803, and before final approval, it will be necessary that the title be traced previous to that year. Yours truly.

As a result, the lawyer sent the following letter to the government:

Gentlemen, your letter regarding title received. I note you wish title to be claimed back further than I have done it.

I was unaware that any educated man failed to know that Louisiana was purchased by the United States from France in 1803. The title of the land was acquired by France by right of conquest of Spain. The land came into possession of Spain in 1492 by right of discovery by a Spanish-Portuguese sailor named Christopher Columbus, who had been granted the privilege of seeking a new route to India by Queen Isabella.

The good queen, being a pious woman and careful about title, took the precaution of securing the blessing of the pope upon Columbus's voyage before she sold her jewels to finance his voyage.

Now the pope, as you know, is the emissary of Jesus Christ, who is the Son of God. And God made the world. Therefore, I believe it is safe to assume that He also made that part of the United States called Louisiana, and I now hope you're satisfied.

✙ ✙ ✙

A pastor at a frontier church ended a moving sermon saying, "All those who want to go to heaven, put up your hands!"

Of course everyone raised their hands, that is; everybody except a rough-looking old cowboy who had been slouching against the doorpost at the back of the room.

All heads turned as he swaggered up to the front, spurs jangling, and drawled, "Preacher, that was too easy. How do you know if these folks are serious? I can prove who really means it and who don't!"

Bemused the preacher said, "Okay, stranger, go ahead and put the faith of these good people to the test."

At that, the cowpoke pulled his twin six-shooters, turned to the audience and said, "Who wants to go to heaven? Raise your hands!"

✙ ✙ ✙

During the French Revolution they condemned a priest and an engineer to be executed by the guillotine. The priest requested that he be executed faceup so he would be looking toward heaven when he died.

The executioner raised the blade of the guillotine and released it. It came speeding down and suddenly stopped, just inches from the priest's neck. The authorities were amazed and took this as divine intervention. The priest was released.

Then the engineer was placed on the guillotine. He also requested to die facing up, thinking maybe he would have the same good fortune as the priest. As the executioner slowly raised the blade of the guillotine, the engineer suddenly exclaimed, "Look—I see what the problem is. . ."

Q: What did the King James Bible say to King James?
A: I have more pages than you!

At a monastery deep in the woods, monks observed a rigid vow of silence. This vow could only be broken once a year on Christmas, by one monk, who could speak only one sentence.

One year, a brother used his turn to speak by saying, "I love the delightful mashed potatoes we have every year with the Christmas roast!" Then he sat down.

Total silence ensued for twelve months until the next Christmas when another brother got his turn. He said, "I think the mashed potatoes are lumpy and disgusting."

Once again, silence ensued for 365 days. The following Christmas, yet another brother rose and said, "This constant arguing makes me ill."

Country Church

"WE'RE RIGHT PLEASED TO ANNOUNCE WE'RE MEET'N OUR BUDGET NOW THAT REV. BEASLEY HAS BEEN RAIS'N CATFISH IN THE BAPISTRY."

You might be in a country church if. . .

- the doors are never locked.
- the call to worship is "Y'all come on in!"
- people still grumble about Noah letting coyotes on the ark.
- when the pastor says, "I'd like to ask Bubba to help take up the offering," five guys stand up.
- the restrooms are outside.
- opening day of deer season is recognized as an official church holiday.
- a member requests to be buried in his four-wheel-drive truck because "I ain't never been in a hole it couldn't get me out of."
- in the annual stewardship drive there is at least one pledge of "two hogs."
- never in its entire 150-year history has one of its pastors had to buy meat or vegetables.

A university professor, vacationing in the country, struck up a conversation with a local. When the prof learned his acquaintance was a country preacher, he asked the man, "Do you honestly believe that Jonah spent three days and three nights in the belly of a huge fish?"

The preacher responded, "I don't know, sir. But when I get to heaven, I'll ask him."

"But just suppose he isn't there?" the professor pressed.

"Then you ask him."

For their pastor's birthday, the little country congregation decided to give him a spiffy new suit. He was so touched that the following Sunday he tearfully announced, "Today I preach to you in my birthday suit."

The pastor of a country church couldn't afford a secretary so he purchased a computer to help get his work done.

Amazed at the labor-saving help it provided, he thought, *This thing is almost human. Though it won't actually be human until it can make a mistake and blame it on another machine!*

An old country pastor who raised chickens happened across a mysterious box in his closet. The box contained three eggs and a thousand one-dollar bills. Amazed, he called his wife to ask her about his find.

Embarrassed, she admitted to having hidden the box their entire forty-five years of marriage. Curious, the pastor asked, "Why would you hide this from me?"

"Oh, I never meant to hurt your feelings," his wife replied.

"What do you mean, hurt my feelings? How could this box hurt my feelings?"

"Well," she responded, "every time I've heard you preach a poor sermon, I put an egg in the box."

The pastor thought that three poor sermons in forty-five years was nothing to feel badly about, so he asked her what the money was for.

His wife replied, "Every time I got a dozen eggs, I sold them to the neighbors for one dollar."

Three city preachers were lost on a country road when they missed a turn and drove into the ditch. As they pulled themselves together, the town drunk pulled up and asked if they were all right.

"Oh, yes, Jesus is with us," one replied.

The Good Samaritan thought that over for a minute. "Well, you'd better let Him get in with me," he said, " 'cuz you're gonna kill Him!"

A young preacher, assigned to a country church, was making visits to his new neighbors.

"Do you belong to the Christian family?" he asked an old farmer.

"No," the man replied, "they live two farms down."

"What I mean is," the preacher continued, "are you lost?"

"No, I've lived here sixty years."

Exasperated, the preacher pressed on. "I mean, are you ready for Judgment Day?"

"When is that?" the farmer asked.

"It could be today or tomorrow!" the preacher exclaimed.

"Well," the farmer replied, "when you find out for sure, let me know. We don't get out much so my wife will probably want to go both days!"

To the search committee of a country congregation, a pastoral candidate said, "If I am voted in as pastor of this church, I will work hard to bring us into the nineteenth century."

A member spoke up. "Uh, Preacher, don't you mean the twenty-first century?"

The pastor replied, "Let's just take it one century at a time."

Three country preachers were discussing their attempts to get rid of the bats in their respective church bell towers.

The first said he had tried to shoot them, but that had left holes in the roof—and now he had leaks as well as bats. The second said he had tried catching the bats in a net and driving them out into the country—but the bats usually returned before he did.

The third preacher announced he had solved the problem. "I baptized them and added them to our membership," he said, "and I haven't seen them since!"

An old country preacher was fishing one afternoon when he noticed a frog sitting next to him. The frog said, "Mister, I've had a spell cast on me. If you'll kiss me, I'll turn into a beautiful princess and I'll make you happy for the rest of your life."

The old preacher smiled, picked up the frog, and put it in his pocket. After a while, he looked into his pocket to see how the frog was doing.

The frog said again, "Mister, I've had a spell cast on me. If you'll kiss me, I'll turn into a beautiful princess and I'll make you happy for the rest of your life."

The preacher just smiled and kept on fishing. When he checked on the frog again, it said, "What's wrong with you, fella? I said I've been bewitched. Just kiss me and I'll turn back into a beautiful princess and make you the happiest man on earth for the rest of your life!"

The old preacher just smiled and said, "Frog, I'm sorry to tell you this. . .but at my age, I'd rather have a talking frog than a beautiful princess!"

The country preacher was explaining the Ten Commandments the best way he knew how to his congregation of farmers and cowboys:

1. Jes' one God.
2. Put nothin' before God.
3. Watch yer mouth.
4. Git yourself to Sunday meetin'.
5. Honor yer ma and pa.
6. No killin'.
7. No foolin' around with another fella's gal.
8. Don't take what ain't yers.
9. No tellin' tales.
10. Don't be hankerin' for yer buddy's stuff.

In rural Alaska's salmon country, a pastor told his congregation, "Jesus says, 'Be ye fishers of men.' All ya gotta do is catch 'em. . .He'll clean 'em!"

A tiny church had been struggling with offerings. One Sunday the pastor announced, "Now, before we pass the collection plate, I'd like to request that whoever stole the chickens from Farmer Hatfield's henhouse please refrain from giving any money to the Lord. God doesn't want money from a thief!"

The church had its best offering in years.

Signs Your Pastor Is a Cowboy at Heart:

- His sermon on Revelation is entitled "Showdown at High Noon."
- He replaces the altar call with the "roundup."
- He refers to deacons' meetings as "campfire chats."
- He walks into the pulpit with a hearty "Hi-Ho Silver!"
- He always refers to his Bible as "My Six-Shooter."
- He tells the ushers to tie bandanas around their faces when taking the offering.
- He begins wedding ceremonies with "Howdy, pardners."
- He constantly threatens to preach well past "high noon."

On a cold, snowy, January Sunday, only the pastor and one farmer arrived at the village church.

"Well, I guess we won't have a service today," the

A preacher was repairing the fence around the old country church. He noticed that a small boy had been watching him for some time.

"Do you want to speak with me, son?" the pastor asked.

"Oh, no," the boy replied. "I'm just waiting."

"Waiting for what?" the preacher asked.

"Waiting to hear what a preacher says when he hits his finger with a hammer!"

pastor said.

To which the farmer replied, "If only one cow shows up at feeding time, I still feed it!"

A group of women were talking during a quilting bee.

"Our congregation is sometimes down to thirty or forty on a Sunday," said the first.

"Oh, that's nothing," the second commented. "Sometimes our congregation is down to a dozen or so."

"It's gotten so bad in our church," the third replied, "that when the minister says 'dearly beloved,' it makes me blush!"

A farmer ran into his pastor after missing the morning service.

"I'm sorry we missed you this morning," the pastor said.

"Well, Reverend, I had some hay to put up," the farmer replied. "I figured it was better to sit on a bale of hay thinking about God than to sit in church thinking about hay!"

The Wednesday night church service coincided with the last day of hunting season. When the pastor asked if anyone had bagged a deer, no one raised a hand.

"I don't get it," the pastor said. "Many of you said you were missing last Sunday because of hunting season, so I had the whole congregation pray for your deer!"

"Well, it worked," one hunter groaned. "They're all safe."

A pastor grew watermelons to supplement his meager income. He was doing all right, but it bothered him that local kids would sneak into his patch at night and eat his melons.

After some thought, he came up with an idea he felt sure would scare the kids away. The pastor made a sign reading, WARNING! ONE OF THESE WATERMELONS HAS BEEN INJECTED WITH RAT POISON! and posted it in the field. Pleased with himself, he went to bed.

The next day, the pastor surveyed his field and found that no watermelons were missing. But there was a sign next to his reading, NOW THERE ARE TWO!

A country preacher and his family were visiting the city for the first time. They were impressed by almost everything they saw, especially the skyscrapers. In the lobby of one tall building, the preacher and his son watched with amazement as two shiny, silver walls slid open before them, revealing a small room behind.

"What is that, Pop?" the boy asked.

"I've never seen anything like it, son," the pastor replied. "I don't know what it is."

At that moment, a stooped old lady shuffled into the tiny room and pressed a button on the wall. The shiny, silver doors closed, and a panel of numbers above the doors lit up—1, 2, 3, all the way to 10.

Then the numbers reversed direction—10, 9, 8, 7,

back to 1. The shiny, silver walls slid open again and a beautiful young woman stepped out.

"Son," the preacher said, staring, "go get your mother."

A young cowboy was explaining to the boys back at the ranch about his first visit to church.

"When I got there, they had me park my truck in the corral," he began.

"You mean the parking lot," interrupted a more worldly wise cowboy.

"I walked up the trail to the door," the first cowboy continued.

"The sidewalk," the second corrected.

"Inside the door, I was met by this dude," the first went on.

"Probably an usher," the second explained.

"Well, the usher led me down the chute," the first said.

"You mean the aisle," the second corrected again.

"Then he had me sit in a stall," the first continued.

"Pew," the second cowboy said.

"Yeah," recalled the first, "that's what that lady beside me said."

A farmer didn't have a chance to unload his truck before church on Sunday. After the service, a little boy saw the big load and asked, "What've you got in your truck?"

"Fertilizer," the farmer replied.

"What are you going to do with it?" the boy asked.

"Put it on strawberries," the farmer answered.

"You ought to come home with us," the boy said. "We put sugar and whipped cream on ours."

A well-known photographer was contracted to illustrate a book on church architecture. So he flew to San Francisco to begin taking pictures, with plans to work his way eastward.

In a large, ornate church, he spotted a golden telephone hung on the wall, with a sign beside it reading $10,000 A MINUTE. Seeking out the pastor, the photographer asked for more information and was told that the golden phone was actually a direct line to heaven. For the stated price, he could talk directly to God.

Continuing on his way, the photographer saw similar golden telephones—and $10,000 A MINUTE signs—in churches in Denver, St. Louis, Chicago, and Detroit.

Dropping southward, the photographer ended up in a tiny church in rural North Carolina. There, he saw the golden telephone—but this time the sign read, CALLS: 25 CENTS. Fascinated, he asked to talk to the pastor.

"Reverend, I've been in cities all across the country and in each church I found this direct line to heaven, for $10,000 a minute. Your sign says it's only a quarter a call. What's the difference?"

"Son, you're in God's country now," the pastor replied. "It's a local call."

A southern preacher thought a visual demonstration would add emphasis to his Sunday sermon. He put a live fishing worm into a jar of alcohol as he began his talk.

While he preached, the worm in the alcohol struggled and died.

"What can we learn from this demonstration?" the pastor asked.

"If you drink, you won't have worms!" someone replied.

A man and his ten-year-old son were out for a fishing weekend, miles from home. At the boy's insistence, they decided to attend the Sunday worship service at a small rural church.

The father was getting short on cash, so he gave his son a dime to drop in the offering plate. In their car after the service, the father complained. "That service was way too long," he lamented. "The sermon was boring, and the singing was off key."

"Dad," the boy replied, "I thought it was pretty good for a dime."

A country preacher was fond of pure, hot horseradish. His wife would regularly make it fresh so he always had a bottle of it with each meal. One night, the pastor offered some to a dinner guest, who took a big spoonful. The man's eyes bulged and his face turned bright red. When he was finally able to speak again, the guest said, "I've heard of pastors who preach hellfire, but you're the first one I've met who passes out samples of it!"

A small rural town hadn't seen rain for weeks. The crops were dying, the fields were brown, and the people's spirits were anxious. When weeks turned to months, the community's three churches called a joint meeting on the town square to pray for rain. The pastors asked the townspeople to bring an object of faith to help inspire the prayers. On the appointed day, everyone showed up to ask God for rain, and the pastors were deeply moved to see the many inspirational objects that were brought along: Bibles, crosses, candles, flowers. But the prayer meeting really got going when a young boy showed up with an umbrella!

A young couple usually sat in the back of their little country church. But one Sunday, running a bit late, they found their usual seats taken. The only spot available was in the second row, to which the usher directed them.

The old church member they sat next to didn't recognize the couple and cheerfully welcomed them. "Good to have ya with us!" he exclaimed. "Where are y'all from?"

Embarrassed, the young man mumbled, "The back."

Just out of seminary, a young man became the pastor of a small rural church. Nervous on his first Sunday, he began his sermon by saying, "I will teach from the passage where Jesus, with five thousand loaves and two thousand fish, feeds five people."

In general, the congregation managed to keep from laughing out loud. But one man couldn't contain himself and let out a huge guffaw, and then continued to snicker throughout the sermon.

The next week the pastor hoped to make a better impression, so he decided to preach a similar message from the same passage.

"This morning I have a similar message as last week," he said. "I am using the story where Jesus, with five loaves and two fish feeds five thousand people."

The pastor looked confidently at the man who had laughed so much the week before. "Now, sir, could you have done that?" he asked.

"Why sure," the man answered, "if I had what was left over from last week."

A country church had a small congregation of faithful people—all but one farmer, who had quit coming to church altogether. The pastor decided to visit the farmer and ask him why he wasn't attending anymore.

"Well, Pastor," the farmer said, "I have only these shabby overalls and worn-out boots. I don't think it's right for me to enter the Lord's house looking this way."

The pastor replied, "Well, I've got an extra suit and shoes that might fit you. I'll give them both to you if you'll come back to church!"

The farmer agreed, so the pastor returned that afternoon with the clothes. The next Sunday the pastor expected to see the farmer but he never showed up. So the minister went out to the farm again and said, "We missed you at church this week. I gave you all of those clothes and I thought you said you would be there. What happened?"

"Well, I got cleaned up and put on all those fancy

clothes of yours," the man replied. "When I passed the mirror, I looked so doggone good I just went to the big city church!"

✝ ✝ ✝

A pastor had been invited for supper at a farmer's home. They had just finished an excellent chicken dinner when the minister saw a rooster strutting through the yard.

"That's certainly a proud-looking rooster," the pastor commented.

"Yes, sir," replied the farmer. "He has every reason to be proud! One of his sons just entered the ministry!"

✝ ✝ ✝

An old country pastor traveled to the city to pray with a congregant who was in the hospital.

It had been some time since the minister had visited the hospital, and he sensed how much things had changed since his last stop. When a technician followed the pastor onto the elevator, wheeling a large machine covered with tubes, wires, and dials, the minister commented, "Boy, would I hate to be hooked up to that thing."

"So would I," replied the technician. "It's an industrial floor cleaner."

✝ ✝ ✝

Just before Thanksgiving, at the only gas station in their tiny town, a pastor waited in a long line. The attendant worked quickly, but there were still many cars ahead of the preacher. Finally, the attendant motioned the pastor toward a vacant pump.

"Hello, Preacher," said the young man. "I'm sorry about the delay. Everyone always waits until the last minute to get ready for a long trip."

"I know what you mean," the pastor replied. "It's the same in my business."

A preacher, newly called to a small country town, needed to mail a letter. Passing a young boy on the street, the pastor asked where he could find the post office. After getting his answer, the minister thanked the boy and said, "If you'll come to the community church this evening, you can hear me tell everyone how to get to heaven."

"I don't know, sir," the boy replied. "You don't even know how to get to the post office!"

A preacher whose members consisted mostly of rural farmers decided to preach a sermon he was sure that everyone would understand. Here are the notes:

A Garden Blessed by God

Plant three rows of peas:
1. "Peas" of heart
2. "Peas" of soul
3. "Peas" of mind

Plant three rows of squash:
1. Squash gossip
2. Squash grumbling
3. Squash selfishness

Plant four rows of lettuce:
1. Lettuce love one another
2. Lettuce be charitable
3. Lettuce be faithful
4. Lettuce not be discouraged

Plant three rows of turnips:
1. Turnip for church each week
2. Turnip to serve in a ministry
3. Turnip to help one another

Plant six rows of thyme:
1. Thyme for the Lord
2. Thyme for your family
3. Thyme for prayer
4. Thyme for work
5. Thyme for rest
6. Thyme for play

Water with patience and cultivate with love. You always reap what you sow.

A preacher was enjoying a meal at the farmhouse of one of his members.

"Your chicken is delicious!" the pastor commented. "How did you prepare it?"

"I didn't do anything special," replied the farmer's

wife. "I just told it straight out that it was going to die."

✛ ✛ ✛

Knock, knock.
Who's there?
Venice.
Venice who?
Venice the potluck going to start?

✛ ✛ ✛

A country church was holding a covered dish supper on the first night of a revival. The guest preacher was invited to lead the food line, but he declined. "I can't eat a big meal before I preach," he said. "It detracts from my ability to deliver a good sermon."

Two hours later, several women were cleaning up the church kitchen. "I declare," grumbled one, "that preacher might as well have ate his fill at suppertime!"

✛ ✛ ✛

In West Virginia's rugged coal country, an old preacher told a boy, "Son, remember that faith can move mountains."

"Yeah," the boy replied, "but dynamite's more exciting!"

✛ ✛ ✛

A flatlander was invited to preach in a Baptist church set in the mountains. He was worried, remembering that the people in this region despised educated preachers and were known for their fundamentalism and simplistic approach to the gospel. He preached with masterful command of allegory and hard truths veiled in simile. At the close of his message he gave the normal invitation. He was amazed to see that an old gentleman in starched overalls responded. Thinking he'd made an impact on the man's heart, he approached him. However, the old man came forward and whispered in the minister's ear, "Young feller, just because the water's muddy, don't mean it's deep!"

One Sunday a student preacher was invited to a church in tobacco country. After his sermon, in which he delivered a hellfire-and-brimstone message against the evils of tobacco, he was approached by the church treasurer. "You should know, this money came from tobacco," the man said, as he held out the check.

The preacher glanced at the check, then took it, saying, "Well, the devil's had it long enough."

A poor country pastor was visiting the city for the first time. Unfortunately, he was accosted by a robber who stuck a gun in the preacher's back.

"One move and you're dead," the bad guy growled. "I'm looking for your money."

"Yeah, me, too," the pastor responded.

Visitors

"I DON'T MEAN TO BE CRITICAL, BUT THAT'S THE COLDEST CHURCH I'VE EVER BEEN TO!"

A young couple was visiting a church for the first time. As the preacher's sermon dragged on, their little girl became restless. Finally, she leaned over to her mother and whispered, "Mommy, if we give him the money now, will he let us go?"

A woman took her four-year-old daughter to church for the first time. Soon, the lights were lowered and the choir came down the aisle, carrying lighted candles. All was hushed until the little girl began to sing, "Happy birthday to you, happy birthday to you!"

A young girl invited a friend to church. The two whispered and giggled throughout much of the sermon. Finally, the girl's older brother had had enough. "You're not supposed to talk in church," he whispered.

"Why?" the little girl replied. "Who's going to stop me?"

The boy pointed to two men standing at the back of the sanctuary. "Those guys," he said, "the hushers."

A little boy was visiting his grandparents' church. As they left, the minister asked the family how they had liked the service. Before the grandparents could speak, the boy blurted out, "I liked the music, but the commercial was too long!"

A young mother was visiting church at Christmastime as the guest of a neighbor. In his message, the pastor described the wise men bringing gifts of gold, frankincense, and myrrh to the infant Jesus. The visitor leaned over to her host and whispered, "A wise *woman* would have brought diapers!"

His marriage in trouble, a man decided to attend church. There, he asked the pastor if they could discuss his marital issues privately.

In a counseling room, the pastor asked several questions to gauge the man's situation, then suggested the man take his wife a gift to show his love.

The visitor shook his head. "What can you give a wife who has everything, yet none of it is paid for?"

The town drunk was visiting church with his equally boozy father. On his way out, they shook the pastor's hand.

"It's good to have you here," the preacher exclaimed. "Have you given up drinking?"

"I don't drink anything stronger than pop," the man replied. Then he clapped his father on the shoulder. "But Pop will drink almost anything!"

✛ ✛ ✛

It was the third time the man had visited the Baptist church. The church's old pastor was good-natured, but he wasn't known for a keen memory.

"Good morning. Is this your first time with us?" the pastor asked the man.

"No, sir," the visitor replied. "It's my third."

"Oh, I'm sorry," the pastor apologized. "I can't seem to remember a name, but I always forget a face!"

✛ ✛ ✛

Visiting for the first time, a family was invited to stay for a church's weekly potluck meal. "I'm glad you've decided to stay," a tablemate told them. "But I need to warn you: The food is usually so bad they serve antacids for dessert!"

✛ ✛ ✛

A visiting preacher gave his hat to the ushers so they could pass it around for a goodwill offering. When it came back to the preacher, it was nearly empty.

But the preacher didn't flinch. He raised the hat to heaven and said, "I thank You, Lord, that I got my hat back from this congregation!"

✛ ✛ ✛

A preacher had had a bad week. On Sunday he was still frustrated and began his sermon by saying, "Every member of this church is in for judgment if you don't change your ways!"

A man in the back of the sanctuary began to laugh. The pastor repeated his warning—and the man continued to laugh. After the service the preacher asked the man why he was laughing.

"Because I don't belong to this church!" was the reply.

Touring New York City, a young family decided to visit Saint Patrick's Cathedral. The kids were especially curious about the votive candles, and the priest asked if they'd each like to light one. The priest explained that it was customary to say a prayer of petition or thanks when lighting and he was careful to tell the kids that votives were not like birthday candles. "Do you have any questions?" he asked.

"No," said the five-year-old. "But if there's a pony outside, it's mine!"

A preacher was using gardening terms to illustrate his message.

"We are a lot like flowers—and God knows just how to make each of us grow," he said. "For example, roses must be planted in the sun but impatiens thrive in the shade."

Afterward, a visitor approached the pastor. "Your sermon did me so much good," she said. "I always wondered what was wrong with my impatiens!"

✚ ✚ ✚

A scruffy man sat in the back of a church. Having never seen the man before, the pastor made a special point of introducing himself.

"We're glad to have you with us," the pastor said. "What brings you here today?"

"Well, my wife sent me," the man replied. "She told me 'Try church. If you don't like it, the devil will always take you back!' "

While on vacation, a devout couple visited a church one Sunday. Since they usually sat close to the front, they made their way to the second row of pews.

Shortly after settling in, an usher tapped the man on the shoulder and whispered, "Excuse me, sir. This pew is saved."

"Well, so are *we*!" the man replied.

✚ ✚ ✚

An usher was escorting worshippers to their seats before the Sunday morning service began. When he asked a visiting couple where they would like to sit, the young man looked confused.

"Nonsmoking, I guess."

In a snobbish, upscale church, an old biker in well-worn boots, jeans, and leather jacket took a seat, only to find that the nattily dressed members of the congregation moved away from him. Throughout the service, the biker felt their looks of disapproval.

Afterward, an usher approached the visitor and said, "Please have a talk with God before you come back. Ask Him what He thinks would be appropriate attire for attending our worship service."

The biker returned the following Sunday in his boots, jeans, and leather jacket. The same usher found the man and said, "I thought I asked you to speak to the Lord before you came back to our church."

"I did," the visitor replied. "He said He doesn't have a clue as to what I should wear here. He's never been here Himself!"

One man attended church so infrequently that people assumed he was a visitor. After one Sunday service, the pastor grabbed him by the hand and pulled him aside.

"Friend, you need to join the army of the Lord!" the pastor said.

The man replied, "I'm already in the army of the Lord, Pastor."

"Then why don't I see you except at Christmas and Easter?" the pastor asked.

The man whispered in response, "I'm in the secret service."

After a Sunday service, a burly visitor asked to speak with the minister's wife who was well-known for her charitable impulses.

"Madam," he said in a broken voice, "I wish to draw your attention to the terrible plight of a poor family in this neighborhood. The father is dead, the mother is too ill to work, and the seven children are starving. They are about to be turned out onto the cold, empty streets unless someone pays their rent—which amounts to $600."

"How terrible!" exclaimed the pastor's wife. "Thank you for bringing this to my attention. May I ask who you are?"

The sobbing visitor applied his handkerchief to his eyes. "I'm the landlord!"

✠ ✠ ✠

"Why are you eating so fast?" a visitor asked during an after-church potluck.

His neighbor replied, "I'm afraid I might lose my appetite before I'm finished!"

"Immediately after the service," the pastor announced, "there will be a meeting of the board."

The sermon concluded, board members gathered at the back of the sanctuary, only to find a stranger in their midst. The man was a first-time visitor.

"Friend," said the pastor, "do you know that this is a meeting of the board?"

"Yes," the visitor replied, "and after today's sermon, I suppose I'm just about as bored as anyone else."

A young boy called a nearby church to ask the pastor to come and pray for his very ill mother. The pastor knew the family had visited his church but was now attending another church down the road.

"I'd be happy to," the pastor replied, "but shouldn't you be asking your new pastor to pray with your mom instead?"

"Well," the boy replied, "we didn't want to take the chance that he might catch whatever it is that Mom has!"

✙ ✙ ✙

At the conclusion of Sunday service, worshippers filed out of the sanctuary and greeted the minister. A young visitor shook the preacher's hand, thanked him for the sermon, and said, "You know, I think you must be smarter than Einstein."

Pleasantly surprised, the minister responded, "Why, thank you!"

As the week went by, the minister began to wonder why anyone would deem him "smarter than Einstein." So he decided that if the visitor returned, he would ask him to explain.

The following Sunday the minister was glad to see the man back in church. After the service, he asked, "Exactly what did you mean when you said that I must be smarter than Einstein?"

"Well, Reverend," the visitor replied, "they say that Einstein was so smart that only ten people in the entire world could understand him. But I'm not sure *anyone* can understand you!"

From a first-time visitor's packet:

- We are friendly. If you are not friendly, out you go!
- We are genuine people. Even our phonies are real phonies.
- We are always sincere even if we have to fake it.
- We believe in tolerance and cannot stand intolerant people.
- We are optimists. Anyone who doesn't look on the bright side depresses us.
- We are more noncompetitive than other groups.
- We believe in equality: Everyone is as good as the next person and a whole lot better.
- We have our critics, but they are paranoid.
- We are prompt about being late to meetings.
- Dogmatism is absolutely forbidden.
- Freedom of belief is rigidly enforced.
- And to this wonderful church we joyfully welcome you!

An elderly woman walked to the sanctuary door where a deacon, serving as usher, greeted her.

"Where would you like to sit?" the deacon asked.

"The front row, please," the woman answered.

"You really don't want to do that," the deacon replied. "The pastor is pretty boring."

The woman's eyes narrowed. "Do you know who I am?" she asked.

"No," he said.

"I'm the pastor's mother!" she replied furiously.

"Do you know who I am?" he asked.

"No," she said.

"Good!" he answered, and ducked out the door.

✚ ✚ ✚

"I hope it didn't disrupt you too badly when my husband walked out during your sermon, Pastor," an embarrassed visitor said as she was leaving church.

"I must admit that it was a little distressing," the preacher replied. "But I'm still glad you both could join us today."

"Please don't take it personally, Pastor," she insisted. "Ron has been walking in his sleep most of his life!"

One Sunday after a sermon about peacemaking, a preacher announced that miniature wooden crosses would be given to each family on the way out.

"Put a cross in the room where your family argues the most," the preacher said. "When you look at the cross, it will remind you about this message and that God is watching."

As people were leaving, a visitor approached the pastor and asked, "Could I have six?"

A church member invited his neighbor to church for the first time. The neighbor noticed that as the pastor got up to preach, he took off his watch and laid it on the pulpit.

"What does that mean?" the neighbor whispered to his host.

"Unfortunately, it doesn't mean anything," the church member replied.

Signs and Bulletins

"UH-OH. . . .I'VE GOT A HUNCH WE SHOULD HAVE PROOFREAD THE BULLETIN THIS MORNING."

Classic Bulletin Bloopers

The spring retreat will be hell May 10 and 11.

The senior choir invites any member of the congregation who enjoys sinning to join the choir.

The pastor spoke briefly, much to the delight of his audience.

Please join us as we show our support for this young couple who are preparing for the girth of their first child.

This afternoon there will be a meeting in the south and north ends of the church. Children will be baptized at both ends.

The pastor will preach his farewell message, after which the choir will sing, "Break Forth with Joy."

Tuesday at 4:00 p.m. there be an ice cream social. All ladies giving milk should come early.

The sermon this morning: "Jesus Walks on the Water." The sermon tonight: "Searching for Jesus."

The outreach committee has enlisted twenty-five members to make calls on people who are not afflicted with any church.

The third verse will be sung without musical accomplishment.

Next Sunday, we will have a soloist for the morning service. Then the pastor will speak about "The Terrible Experience."

Ladies, don't forget the rummage sale. It is a good chance to get rid of those things not worth keeping around the house. Bring your husbands.

The agenda was adopted. The minutes were approved. The financial secretary gave a grief report.

Our dear brother has gone on to be the Lord.

Candle-lighting directions: 1. The pastor will light his candle from the altar candles. 2. The ushers will light their candle from the pastor's candle. 3. The ushers will turn and light each worshipper in the first pew.

If you choose to heave during the postlude, please do so quietly.

The Newly Marrieds are now having Bile studies each Tuesday evening at 7:30 p.m.

At the evening service tonight, the sermon topic will be "What Is Hell?" Come early, and listen to our choir practice.

The class on prophecy has been canceled due to unforeseen circumstances.

Due to the rector's illness, Wednesday's healing services will be discontinued until further notice.

The young couple requests your presents at their wedding.

There is a sign-up sheet for anyone wishing to be baptized on the table in the foyer.

A new loudspeaker system has been installed in the church. It was given by one of our members in memory of his wife.

There is joy in heaven over one singer who repents.

The ladies of the church have cast off clothing of every kind, and they can be seen in the church basement on Friday afternoon.

Pastor is on vacation. Massages can be given to the church secretary.

Ushers will eat latecomers.

Scouts are saving aluminum cans, bottles, and other items to be recycled. Proceeds will be used to cripple children.

Attend and you will hear an excellent speaker and heave a healthy lunch.

The dieting support group will meet at 7:00 p.m. Please use large double door at the side entrance.

The peacemaking meeting scheduled for today has been canceled due to a conflict.

Hymn No. 58—"Gold Will Take Care of You"

Don't let worry kill you—let the church help.

Today's Sermon: How Much Can a Man Drink? with Hymns from a Full Choir.

Hymn No. 262—"Immoral, Invisible"

Remember in prayer the many who are sick of our community.

The church will host an evening of fine dining, superb entertainment, and gracious hostility.

The "Over 60s Choir" will be disbanded for the summer with the thanks of the entire church.

The cost for attending the Fasting and Prayer conference includes meals.

Smile at someone who is hard to love. Say "hell" to someone who doesn't care much about you.

The soloist sang "I Will Not Pass This Way Again," giving obvious pleasure to the congregation.

For those of you who have children and don't know it, we have a nursery downstairs.

Next Thursday there will be tryouts for the choir. They need all the help they can get.

Mrs. Ross remains in the hospital and needs blood donors for more transfusions. She is also having trouble sleeping and requests tapes of the pastor's sermons.

During the absence of our pastor, we enjoyed the rare privilege of hearing a good sermon when Reverend White supplied our pulpit.

The couple was married on June 24 in the church. So ends a friendship that began in their school days.

Six new choir robes are currently needed,
due to the addition of several new members
and to the deterioration of some older ones.

A bean supper will be held on Wednesday evening in the church hall. Music will follow.

Potluck dinner Sunday at 5:00 p.m. Prayer and medication to follow.

This evening at 6:00 p.m. there will be a hymn sing in the park across from the church. Bring a blanket and come prepared to sin.

The pastor's wife would appreciate it if the ladies of the congregation would lend her their electric girdles for the pancake breakfast next Sunday.

Low Self-Esteem Support Group will meet Wednesday at 6:00 p.m. Please use the back door.

The youth group will be presenting Shakespeare's *Hamlet* in the Fellowship Hall Friday at 7:00 p.m. The congregation is invited to attend this tragedy.

Evening massage—6:00 p.m.

Stewardship offertory: "Jesus Paid It All"

The concert held in the Fellowship Hall was a great success. Special thanks are due to the pastor's wife, who labored the whole night at the piano, which, as usual, fell upon her.

Fifteen members were present at the church meeting held at the home of Mrs. Brown last night. Two ladies sang a duet, "The Lord Knows Why."

The songfest was hell at the Methodist church on Wednesday.

Next Saturday is the family hayride and bonfire. Bring your own hot dogs and guns. Friends are welcome! Everyone come for a fun time.

When parking on the north side of the church, please remember to park on an angel.

This being Easter Sunday, we will ask Mrs. Potter to come forward and lay an egg on the altar.

The church office will be closed until opening. It will remain closed after opening. It will reopen Monday.

On Sunday a special collection will be taken to help pay for the new carpet. All those wishing to do something on the new carpet should please come forward.

A member has volunteered to strip and refinish the communion table in the sanctuary.

The visiting monster today is Reverend Wilson.

Volunteers are needed to spit up food for distribution to local families in need.

Don't forget about Drug Awareness Week: Get involved in drugs before your children do.

Illiterate? Write to the church office for help.

ANOINTING OF THE SICK: If you are going to be hospitalized due to surgery, please contact the pastor. Special prayer also for those who are seriously sick by request.

Please welcome our guest pastor, a caring individual who loves hurting people.

Our annual church picnic will be held this Saturday afternoon. If it rains, it will be held in the morning.

A cookbook is being compiled by women's ministries. Please submit your favorite recipe and a short antidote for it.

The senior pastor will be away for three weeks. The staff members during his absence you will find pinned to the church bulletin board.

Our pastor will be on vacation until the middle of the month. Local clergy will be celebrating on the Sundays when he is away.

Mr. Bates was elected and has accepted the office of head deacon. We could not get a better man.

Are you 55 and getting nowhere? Why not consider the Christian ministry?

Visitors are asked to sing their names at the church entrance.

The youth group is preparing a pizza dinner. It will be held in the perish hall.

The maintenance of the church graveyard is becoming very expensive. It would be a great help if church members would do their best to tend their own graves.

The Women's Ministry will be selling their new cookbook at the church supper this Wednesday night. Proceeds will help purchase a stomach pump for the local hospital.

The church is glad to have with us today as our guest speaker the Reverend Green and his family. After the service we request that all remain in the sanctuary for the Hanging of the Greens.

We need ten more volunteers for summer camp. There will be sinning and dancing.

Seen on the Sign

✚✚✚

SIGN BROKEN—MESSAGE INSIDE THIS SUNDAY

✚✚✚

A CLOSED MOUTH GATHERS NO FOOT

✚✚✚

WALK WITH JESUS—IT'S CHEAPER THAN GAS

✚✚✚

HOW WILL YOU SPEND ETERNITY—SMOKING OR NONSMOKING?

✚✚✚

WHEN YOU SMILE YOU SPOIL THE DAY FOR SOME GROUCH

✚✚✚

GOD SO LOVED THE WORLD THAT HE DID NOT SEND A COMMITTEE

✚✚✚

Beat the Easter Rush—Come to Church This Sunday

✚✚✚

Men's Hearts Are Like Dirty Diapers—They Need Changing

✚✚✚

Don't Wait for the Hearse to Take You to Church

✚✚✚

If You Don't Like the Way the Cookie Crumbles, Try the Bread of Life

✚✚✚

When God Calls Us, Does He Get a Busy Signal?

✚✚✚

To Stay Out of Debt, Act Your Wage

✚✚✚

Nothing Ruins the Truth Like Stretching It

Free Trip to Heaven—Details Inside!

True Christians Can Give Their Parrot to the Town Gossip

No Perfect People Allowed

If You Can't Sleep, Don't Count Sheep. Talk to the Shepherd.

God Believes in Atheists

A Dam Holds Back Water. It's Not My Name.—God

Wonder What Goes on Here Between Weddings and Funerals?

THE GREAT OAK WAS ONCE A NUT THAT STOOD ITS GROUND

SIN HAS NO MINIMUM WAGE

CHRIST IS RISEN. ELEVATOR ENTRANCE TO LEFT.

THE CHURCH IS NOT FULL OF HYPOCRITES. THERE'S STILL ROOM FOR MORE.

Seen outside a parochial school:
REPORT CARD DAY FRIDAY. PRAY FOR PEACE.

From the Bible

NOAH TAKES A LUNCH BREAK...

"CAN YOU BELIEVE THIS. . .ANIMAL CRACKERS!"

Overheard on Noah's ark:

- "Did anyone think about bringing a couple of umbrellas?"
- "Hey, there are more than two flies in here!"
- "Wasn't someone supposed to bring some shovels?"
- "Okay, who's the wise guy who let the mosquitoes on board?"
- "Don't make me pull this ark over and come back there!"
- "And whatever you do, *do not* pull out this plug."
- "Are we there yet?"

Women of the Bible:

- Eve: "Adam, you never take me anywhere different to eat!"
- Elizabeth: "John, I cook you nice meals—but all you want is locust, locust, locust!"
- Pharaoh's daughter: "Moses, stop parting the bath water, and wash behind those ears!"
- David's mom: "He's going to put someone's eye out with that sling!"
- Samson's mom: "Will you please clean the drain after you shampoo?"
- Mary: "Joseph, I told you we should have made reservations!"

Eve never had to listen to Adam talk about how well his mother cooked.

Q: What kind of man was Boaz before he married?
A: Ruthless.

Q: Who was the greatest male financier in the Bible?
A: Noah. He was floating his stock while everyone else was in liquidation.

Q: Who was the greatest female financier in the Bible?
A: Pharaoh's daughter. She went down to the bank of the Nile and drew out a little prophet.

Q: What kind of motor vehicles are in the Bible?
A: Jehovah drove Adam and Eve out of the garden in a Fury. David's Triumph was heard throughout the land. Also, probably a Honda, because the apostles were all in one Accord.

Q: Who was the greatest comedian in the Bible?
A: Samson. He brought the house down.

Q: What excuse did Adam give to his children as to why he no longer lived in Eden?
A: Your mother ate us out of house and home.

Q: Which servant of God was the most flagrant lawbreaker in the Bible?
A: Moses. He broke all Ten Commandments at once.

Q: Which area of Palestine was especially wealthy?
A: The area around Jordan. The banks were always overflowing.

Q: Who is the greatest babysitter mentioned in the Bible?
A: David. He rocked Goliath to a very deep sleep.

✛✛✛

Q: Which Bible character had no parents?
A: Joshua, son of Nun.

✛✛✛

Q: Why didn't they play cards on the ark?
A: Because Noah was standing on the deck. (Groan. . .)

✛✛✛

Q: What did Adam and Eve do after they were kicked out of Eden?
A: They raised Cain.

✛✛✛

The Search for a Pastor During Bible Times

Dear Member,
We do not have a happy report, as we have not been able to find a suitable candidate for pastor of our church thus far. We do, however, have one promising prospect. The following is our confidential report on the candidates:

Adam: Good man, but has problems with his wife.
Noah: Former pastorate of 120 years with no converts. Prone to unrealistic building projects.
Joseph: A big thinker, but a braggart. Interprets dreams. Has a prison record.
Moses: Modest and meek, but poor communicator;

even stutters at times. Sometimes blows his stack and acts rashly in business meetings.

Deborah: One word—*female*.

David: The most promising candidate of all, until we discovered the affair he had with a neighbor's wife.

Solomon: Great preacher, but serious woman problems.

Elijah: Prone to depression; collapses under pressure.

Jonah: Told us he was swallowed by a huge fish. He said the fish later spit him out on the shore near here. We hung up.

Amos: Backward and unpolished. With some seminary training, he might have promise; but he has a problem with wealthy people.

John: Says he's a Baptist, but doesn't dress like one. Sleeps in the outdoors, has a weird diet, and provokes denominational leaders.

Paul: Powerful CEO type and fascinating preacher. But he's short on tact, unforgiving with young ministers, harsh, and has been known to preach all night.

Timothy: Too young.

Judas: His references are solid. A steady plodder. Conservative. Good connections. Knows how to handle money. We're inviting him to preach this Sunday with great hopes that he will accept our offer!

Never let your worries get the best of you. Always remember: Moses started out as a basket case!

God called down to Moses and said, "I've got good news and bad news. Which do you want first?"

Moses replied, "Most merciful Lord, please give me the good news first."

"Well, Moses, the good news is that I've chosen you to deliver my people from bondage," God answered. "I will force Pharaoh to release my children by causing years of pestilence in Egypt. There will be plagues of locusts and frogs and inconceivable devastation upon the land. Pharaoh's armies will chase you as you try to leave, but do not fear because I will part the waters of the Red Sea to aid in your escape."

"And the bad news, Lord?" Moses inquired.

God answered, "You will have to prepare the environmental impact statement."

Moses: "How are we going to get across the sea? The Egyptians are close behind us!"

General of the army: "Normally, I'd recommend that we build our own bridge to carry us across. But there's not enough time for that."

Admiral of the navy: "Normally, I'd recommend that we build barges to carry us across. But time is too short."

Public relations officer: "I don't have a solution, but I can promise you this: If you can find a way out of here, I'll get you two or three pages in the Old Testament!"

✚ ✚ ✚

The former president of the United States was making a public appearance when a man at the edge of the crowd caught his attention. The man had long, flowing white hair, a long white beard, and wore a long white robe. He held a staff in one hand and some stone tablets under the other arm. The president, struck by the man's appearance, told his Secret Service detail, "I want to talk to that man."

Agents cleared a path to the man and the president asked him, "Aren't you Moses?"

The man ignored the president, turning his head to the other side.

Unaccustomed to such treatment, the president moved to position himself in the man's line of sight and asked again, "Hey—aren't you Moses?"

The man continued to turn his head to the other side.

Frustrated, the president tugged the man's sleeve and demanded, "I said, aren't you Moses?"

Finally, the man answered quietly, "Yes, I am."

"Why have you been ignoring me?" the president asked.

The man replied, "Well, the last time I spoke to a *bush* I had to spend forty years in the desert!"

The Bible tells us that we should love our neighbors and our enemies. . .probably because they are usually the same people.

Q: What time of day was Adam created?
A: Just a little before Eve.

Forbidden fruits produce many jams.

The good Lord didn't create anything without a purpose, but mosquitoes have to come pretty close.

Knock, knock.
    Who's there?
    Babylon.
    Babylon who?
    Babylon if you must. I'm not listening.

How long did Cain detest his brother?
    As long as he was Abel.

Knock, knock.
    Who's there?
    Noah.
    Noah who?
    Noah don't know who you are.

Which animals were the last to leave the ark?
    The elephants. It took some time for them to pack their trunks.

Q: Did all the animals on the ark come in pairs?
A: The worms probably came in the apples.

Q: What animal couldn't Noah trust?
A: The cheetah.

Q: Did Noah carry money into the ark?
A: Sure. . .bucks and doe.

Q: Where is the first meat mentioned in the Bible?
A: When Noah took Ham into the ark.

Q: Which animal had the highest level of intelligence on Noah's ark?
A: The giraffe.

Q: Why did Noah have to discipline the chickens on the ark?
A: Because they were using fowl language.

As the Bible tells us, it is much more blessed to give than to receive. That way you don't have to write any thank-you notes, either!

A rat and a mouse were talking on Noah's ark.
"I can't stand this place," said the rat.
"I know," replied the mouse. "I just saw two cockroaches."

Q: Who was the first tennis player in the Bible?
A: Joseph. He served in Pharaoh's court.

Q: Who was most sorry when the prodigal son returned home?
A: The fatted calf.

Sunday school teacher: What does the Bible have to say about the Dead Sea?
Student: Dead? I didn't even know it was sick!

Q: What kind of light did Noah have on the ark?
A: Floodlight.

Q: Who was the fastest runner in history?
A: Adam. He was first in the human race.

Q: What did Noah do for a living?
A: He was an ark-itect.

Q: Where do we find baseball in the Bible?
A: Genesis 1:1: "In the big inning. . ."

Q: Is baseball mentioned in the Bible?
A: Sure! In the big inning, Cain struck out Abel, and the prodigal son came home.

God decided it wasn't good for Adam to be alone, so the Lord visited the man to say, "Adam, I have a plan to fulfill your every need. I'm going to make you happy with a companion who is beautiful and faithful, who will make you feel wonderful every day of your life."

Adam was amazed at the thought. "That sounds great, Lord!"

"I should warn you, though," God replied, "it won't come cheaply. This will cost you an arm and a leg."

"That much?" Adam responded. "What could I get for a rib?"

Adam: "God, why did you make Eve's hair so long and silky?"
God: "So you would like her."
Adam: "And God, why did you make her skin so soft and nice to touch?"
God: "So you would like her."
Adam: "But God, couldn't you have made her a little smarter?"
God: "Well, I wanted her to like you!"

Adam to Eve: "Please quit putting my shirt in the salad!"

Q: Who was the strongest man in the Bible?
A: Jonah. Even a whale couldn't keep him down!

Q: Why was Job always freezing in bed?
A: Because he had awful comforters.

Q: What is the sharpest tool in the New Testament?
A: The Acts of the Apostles

Q: What did the well-mannered sheep say to the other animals in line to get on the ark?
A: "After ewe!"

Q: What did Noah say to the frogs?
A: "Hop on in!"

Q: What did Noah say to the toads?
A: "Wart's new?"

Q: What animals spent most of the time on their knees while on the ark?
A: Birds of prey.

Q: What did Noah's wife have to do with snakes on the ark?
A: As little as possible.

Q: What did Noah call the gorilla's wife?
A: His prime-mate.

Q: What did Noah feed the 500-pound gorilla?
A: Anything it wanted.

Q: Why did some of the snakes disobey Noah when he
told them to "Go forth and multiply"?
A: They couldn't. They were adders.

"Why are the skunks always arguing?" Noah's wife
asked.
"Oh, they just like to make a stink," Noah replied.

Knock, knock.
    Who's there?
    Megan.
    Megan who?
    Megan a joyful noise unto the Lord

✠ ✠ ✠

Knock, knock.
    Who's there?
    Elizabeth.
    Elizabeth who?
    Elizabeth of faith is all you need.

✠ ✠ ✠

Knock, knock.
    Who's there?
    Bolivia.
    Bolivia who?
    Bolivia in the Lord and you shall be saved.

✠ ✠ ✠

Knock, knock.
    Who's there?
    June.
    June who?
    June know the books of the Bible?

✠ ✠ ✠

Knock, knock.
    Who's there?
    Stu.
    Stu who?
    Stu late for Judas, but not for you.

Knock, knock.
   Who's there?
   Sam Day.
   Sam Day who?
   Sam Day we will all meet Jesus.

Q: What's the first court case mentioned in the Bible?
A: Joshua Judges Ruth.

Q: How should you study the New Testament?
A: You Luke into it.

Q: Did Eve ever have a date with Adam?
A: No, most people think it was an apple.

Q: How did Adam and Eve feel while they were getting expelled from the garden?
A: They were really put out.

✝ ✝ ✝

Q: What season was it when Eve ate the fruit?
A: Early in the fall.

✝ ✝ ✝

Q: What do people today have that Adam didn't?
A: Ancestors.

✝ ✝ ✝

Abraham decided to upgrade his old computer to the new version of Windows. Isaac couldn't believe it.

"Dad, your old PC doesn't have enough memory!"

"My son," Abraham responded, "God Himself will provide the RAM."

✝ ✝ ✝

A teacher asked her students to draw a picture of any Old Testament story that they remembered during Sunday school. As she moved around the class, she saw there were many wonderful drawings. Then she came across a boy who had drawn an old man driving what looked like a station wagon. In the back seat were two passengers without any clothes on.

"It's a lovely picture," said the teacher, "but which story does it tell?"

The boy replied. "Doesn't it say in the Bible that God drove Adam and Eve out of the garden of Eden?"

A Sunday school teacher was carefully explaining the story of Elijah the prophet and the false prophets of Baal. She explained how Elijah built an altar and put wood on it, then cut a steer in pieces and laid it on the altar. Then Elijah commanded the people of God to fill four barrels of water and pour it over the altar.

"Now," said the teacher, "can anyone in the class tell me why the Lord would have Elijah pour water over the steer on the altar?"
A little girl raised her hand eagerly and said, "To make the gravy!"

"Does anyone remember anything we learned about Solomon?" a Sunday school teacher asked.

"He had three hundred wives and seven hundred porcupines," a little boy answered.

Boy 1: "My father has Benjamin Franklin's pen."
   Boy 2: "Big deal! My dad has Adam's apple."

"Honey, can you give me a hand with the dishes?" the wife asked.

"I'm no good in the kitchen, my dear," the husband answered. "Besides, that's not a man's work."

"Well, the Bible says that it is!" replied the wife.

"Where?" the man asked suspiciously.

"Second Kings 21:13 says 'And I will wipe Jerusalem as a man wipeth a dish, wiping it and turning it upside down.' "

Did you know that Daniel played a role in closing the mouths of the hungry beasts in the lion's den? Seems that an angel from heaven told Daniel to whisper this into each lion's ear: "After dinner, we'll have speeches."

Weddings

"THESE VOWS WERE WRITTEN BY THE BRIDE AND GROOM AND DO NOT NECESSARILY REFLECT THE VIEWS AND OPINIONS OF THIS CHURCH OR ITS AFFILIATES."

A young boy had been invited to participate in his aunt's wedding. As he walked down the aisle, he would take two steps, stop, and turn, raising his hands like claws and letting out a roar. All the way to the front of the church he followed the pattern: Step, step, *roar!* Step, step, *roar!*

Guests were trying to contain their laughter as the boy reached the platform. When the minister asked what he was doing, the boy replied, "I was just being the ring bear."

A young couple, madly in love, decided to get married. But as the wedding day neared, both grew increasingly nervous over secret problems they had never shared with anyone. Privately, the groom-to-be approached his minister.

"I'm really concerned about this marriage," the young man said.

"Don't you love her?" the pastor asked in surprise.

"Of course," the groom said. "But I have unbelievably smelly feet—and I'm afraid my fiancée won't be able to stand them."

"Oh, is that all?" the pastor replied. "Look, all you need to do is wash your feet twice a day and wear socks all the time."

The groom thought it over and decided it just might work.

Meanwhile, the nervous bride had privately approached the minister's wife. "I'm so worried," she sobbed. "I have really bad breath when I wake up each day!"

"Oh, dear," the pastor's wife replied, "everyone has bad breath in the morning. Don't worry about it."

"No, you don't understand," the bride implored. "My morning breath is so awful, my fiancé won't even want to be near me!"

"Well, I have an idea," the pastor's wife said soothingly. "Set your alarm just a few minutes before your husband wakes up. Run to the bathroom, brush your teeth, and gargle with mouthwash before he gets out of bed. The key is not to say anything until you've taken care of your breath."

The bride thought it over and decided it just might work.

In time, a beautiful wedding was held and the bride and groom enjoyed the day without once worrying about their secret problems. For several months they managed to keep their issues to themselves. Then one morning, the husband awoke before dawn to find that one of his socks had come off in the night. Frantic, he searched the bed, afraid of what might happen if he didn't find his sock soon. His bride awoke with a start, and, without thinking, blurted out, "What in the world are you doing?"

"Oh, dear!" the young man wailed. "You swallowed my sock!"

A young couple called their local church to ask if the pastor could marry them. He agreed, but only if they would work through a few sessions of premarital counseling. On the first visit, the young man, who had never been to church before, was quite nervous. Filling out a questionnaire, the young man read, "Are you entering this marriage of your own free will?" and his mind went totally blank. He looked to his girlfriend for help, and she whispered, "Put down 'yes.' "

✤ ✤ ✤

On their wedding day, a bride and groom are standing at the altar when she catches a glimpse of his golf club bag near the sanctuary exit.

"What in the world are you doing with those clubs at our wedding?" she whispers.

"Well," he responds, "this isn't going to take all afternoon, is it?"

A pompous young man was tired of the way brides got all the attention at weddings. So he decided to write the wedding announcement himself and rush it off to the newspaper. This is what was printed:

Mr. Eric Smith, son of Mr. and Mrs. Robert Smith, became the bridegroom of Miss Heather Jones today at the First Baptist Church. Mr. Smith was attended by his brother John as best man. He was attractively dressed in a tuxedo the color of midnight with matching bow tie. Cut from high-quality wool, this three-button, nonvented black pinstripe tuxedo was classic and sophisticated. Its front besom pockets added an elegant flair while the matching pleated pants oozed with panache. The groom's pants were suspended from the waist, falling in a straight line almost to the floor. On his feet was a pair of magnificent matching shoes revealing just a glimpse of black leather, laced with string in a color that matched the suit. The effect was rather stunning. The best man's attire looked similar to the groom's, and you could sense a hush of admiration come over the crowd as they were awed by the striking display of masculinity. The groom spoke his vows in low but firm tones.

As the bride led the groom from the nuptials, it was noted that she wore the traditional white dress and matching veil.

✚✚✚

During a play date, a mother checked on her daughter and friends and overheard them playing wedding. The vows went like this:

"You have the right to remain silent, anything you say can and will be held against you, you have the right to an attorney. You may kiss the bride."

✚✚✚

"How was the wedding?" a preacher's wife asked.

"It went really well," the preacher replied. "That is, until I asked the bride if she would obey. The bride said, 'Do you think I'm insane?' and the groom said, 'I do,' and it all went downhill from there!"

✚✚✚

A newly married couple was having their first fight. Both husband and wife were red-faced and yelling. After a while, the husband shouted, "When we got married, you promised to love, honor, and obey me!"

"I know I did, but I didn't mean it!" she yelled in return. "What was I supposed to say? Did you want me to start an argument in front of all those people?"

A young girl was attending her first wedding, watching the proceedings with interest for a while before growing restless. The groom stood at the altar as six bridesmaids walked slowly up the aisle, one by one. Soon, the girl leaned over to her mom and whispered, "Why doesn't he just hurry up and pick one?"

A young couple was completing their last session of premarital counseling. The groom-to-be was stumped on this question: "The Bible teaches us to have only one spouse. What is this called?"

After a few minutes of thinking, he wrote down, "Monotony."

Attending her first wedding, a little girl whispered to her mother, "Why is the bride dressed in all white?"

"Because white symbolizes happiness, and today is the happiest day of her life," her mother replied.

The little girl thought for a moment, then asked, "So why is the groom wearing black?"

A bride-to-be went to the jewelry shop to have her prospective groom's ring engraved. She couldn't decide what to say, so she asked the salesperson for advice.

"I want something that has meaning and will remind

him of me," the bride-to-be said.

"How about, 'Put it back on!' "

A family crossing the U.S.-Mexico border for the first time was asked by a customs agent, "What is the purpose of your visit?"

"We're going to a wedding," the mother replied.

"Are you carrying any weapons? Any knives or guns?" the agent asked.

"No," the woman replied, stunned. "It's not that kind of wedding!"

A disc jockey at a wedding reception polled the guests to see who had been married the longest. Finding a couple who'd been married more than fifty years, the entertainer asked the wife, "What advice would you give to the newly married couple?"

"The three most important words in a marriage are, 'You're probably right,' " the woman replied.

The DJ then asked the same of the husband.

"She's probably right," he sighed.

During her daughter's wedding, the mother of the bride had managed to keep from crying until the very end of the ceremony. But at that point, she glanced around and noticed an elderly couple sitting a few rows back on the groom's side. The wife had reached over to her husband's wheelchair and gently touched his hand and that was all it took to start the mother's tears flowing.

After the ceremony, the mother found the couple and told the woman how that tender gesture had tugged at her heart.

"Well, I'm sorry to spoil your moment," the elderly lady replied. "I was just checking to see if he was awake."

At his wedding reception, a groom decided to play a song for his bride on the guitar. But he found that tuning the instrument's strings was taking longer than usual. "Sorry, I'm just not used to this," the groom said. "It's a little harder to do with a ring on."

Just then a man's voice called out, "Everything's harder to do with a ring on!"

A bride-to-be and her mother went shopping to find the mother a dress for the wedding. The women returned a few hours later with ten new dresses.

"Ten!" her husband shouted. "What could any woman possibly want with ten new dresses?"

Smiling, the wife replied, "Ten new pairs of shoes."

"Daddy, how much does it cost to get married?" a girl asked.

"I don't know, honey," the father answered. "I'm still paying for it."

An older widow and widower fell in love and decided to have a simple wedding at a local church. The minister was asked to officiate at their wedding at the close of the morning service.

After the benediction the minister realized he could not remember the names of the couple who were to be married, so he made an announcement: "Will those wanting to get married please come to the front?"

Immediately, nine single women, three widows, four widowers, and a teenaged boy came forward.

wedding celebrates when a man and woman become one. The trouble starts when they try to decide which one.

A minister was called to a nursing home to perform a wedding. An elderly man met him at the door. He seemed quite anxious. The minister sat down to counsel the old man and asked several questions.

"Is she a Christian?" asked the minister.

"I don't know for sure," the elderly man answered.

"Do you love her?"

"I guess," the elderly man replied.

"Well, why are you marrying her?" the minister asked.

"Because she can drive at night."

A young couple who had just graduated from college decided to get married. During premarital counseling, the pastor asked about their relationship.

"We've got a great relationship," the bride-to-be explained. "He was a communications major in college and I majored in theater. He communicates really well and I just act like I'm listening."

A bride and groom had asked the bakery to inscribe their wedding cake with a Bible verse, 1 John 4:18. It reads, "There is no fear in love, but perfect love casts out fear."

The cake decorator, however, misread the reference and instead beautifully inscribed John 4:18 on the cake: "For you have had five husbands, and the man you now have is not your husband."

Weddings have become so expensive that instead of the bride's mother, now it's the bride's father who breaks down and cries!

"Why doesn't anyone ever give the groom a shower?" someone asked at a wedding.

"Because he'll be in hot water soon enough!" an older man replied with a chuckle.

A four-year-old girl couldn't quite grasp the concept of marriage when her father explained it to her. The dad thought some visuals might help, so he pulled out his wedding photo album. One page after another, he pointed out the bride arriving at the church, walking down the aisle, stating her vows, and enjoying the reception.

"Now do you understand?" her father asked.

"I think so," the daughter replied. "That's when Mommy came to work for us, right?"

During a wedding rehearsal, the groom approached the preacher with an unusual offer: "I'll give you $100 if you'll just change the wedding vows slightly. When you get to the part where I'm supposed to 'forsake all others' I'd like you to leave that part out."

The groom tucked the cash into the preacher's Bible and walked away satisfied. But the next day at the wedding, the preacher looked the young man in the eye and said, "Will you promise to love and cherish your lovely bride, to serve her breakfast in bed every morning, and promise that you will not ever even look at another woman, as long as you both shall live?"

The groom gulped as all eyes in the sanctuary awaited his response.

"Yes," he mumbled.

Later, at the reception, the groom cornered the preacher. "I thought we had a deal!" he whispered through clenched teeth.

The preacher put the $100 back in the groom's hand and said, "Your wife made me a much better offer."

"My boyfriend is so original!" said a young girl swooning over the love of her life. "He says things to me that no one else would ever even think of saying."

"What?" replied her brother. "Did he ask you to marry him?"

"WE ARE PLEASED TO ANNOUNCE BEN AND MARTHA'S UPCOMING WEDDING. IF YOU WISH TO BRING GIFTS, THEY ARE REGISTERED AT McGRAFF'S PHARMACY."

The bride was terribly anxious about making a mistake during her wedding ceremony. But the minister reassured her, pointing out that the order of service was not difficult to remember.

"All you have to keep in mind," the minister said, "is that when you enter the church you walk up the *aisle*. The groom and best man will be waiting before the *altar*. Then I shall request the congregation to sing a *hymn*. Then we shall get on with the ceremony. Just remember this order and you can't go wrong!"

The happy day finally arrived, and the bridegroom waited nervously for his bride to appear. As she took her place beside him, he was curious, then horrified, to hear her repeating, "Aisle, altar, hymn. Aisle, altar, hymn. Aisle, altar, hymn. . ."

At her wedding, she got a new name and a dress.

"I dreamed last night that I asked you to marry me," a young man said to his girlfriend. "What do you think that means?"

"It means you've got more sense in your sleep than you do when you're awake!" replied his girlfriend.

"I would like to ask for your daughter's hand in marriage, sir," a young man nervously said to his girlfriend's father. "Do you have any objections?"

"None at all!" said the father. "Take the hand that's always in my pocket."

"Cheer up, son! There are other fish in the sea," a father said to his son a week after his fiancée broke off their engagement.

"Yes, but this last one took all my bait!" cried his son.

"I hope you realize what a generous and giving person you are marrying," the bride's father said to the groom.

"I do, sir!" said the groom. "And I hope she inherited those fine qualities from her father."

A young girl sat alone in a coffee shop nervously twiddling with her coffee cup.

"Is anything wrong, miss?" asked the owner of the coffee shop. "You look pretty worried over something."

"Oh, I'm just trying to decide if I should go to a wedding tomorrow."

"Oh yeah?" the owner asked. "Who's getting married?"

"ME!" she answered.

"There are an awful lot of girls who don't want to get married these days," a young man complained to his father.

"How do you know that?" asked his father.

"Because I've asked them!" replied the young man.

"Honey, have you asked my father if you can marry me yet?" asked the girlfriend.

"No," said her boyfriend. "Whenever I walk into his office I get nervous. I let him pull another tooth today!"

"Don't you want to meet my father before you propose?" a young man's girlfriend asked just as he was about to pop the question.

"Well, I don't know," the young man replied. "Couldn't you just describe him to me?"

An elderly woman, whose previous husbands had all passed away, was getting married for the fourth time. After the ceremony someone asked what she could possibly need with four husbands.

The woman replied, "One for the money, two for the show, three to get ready, and the fourth to go!"

A school-aged boy had just attended his first wedding. After the ceremony his mother asked what he thought of it.

"I was kinda surprised that the preacher said you can marry up to sixteen women!" the boy said.

"What do you mean?" his mother asked in shock.

"I added it up. He said four better, four worse, four richer, four poorer," replied the boy.

"Do you really love me, honey?" the bride asked the groom at the reception.

"You know I do, my dear!" he replied.

"Would you even die for me?" the bride asked.

"No, honey. Mine is an undying love!" he answered.

"Where can I get a license?" a young man asked the clerk.

"A hunting license?" the clerk asked.

"No, the hunt is over," the young man replied. "I want a license to marry the girl I caught."

"Doesn't the bride look stunning?" a wedding guest asked her husband.

"Yes, and doesn't the groom look stunned?" he replied.

An old man was greeted at a wedding by an usher in a tuxedo.

"Are you the groom?" the old man asked.

"No, sir," the young man replied. "I was eliminated in the semifinals."

"Do you think your father will object to me marrying you?" asked a young man.

"I'm not sure," the girl replied. "But if he's anything like me, he will!"

"You seem like a beautiful and smart woman," said a man. "We should get married."

"I don't think so," replied the woman. "I'm just as beautiful and smart as I look."

A young man got down on one knee and said to his girl: "I've been wanting to ask you something for weeks."

"And I've had the answer ready for months!" his girl replied.

An elderly couple got married and went on their honeymoon. They were both in their late eighties.

"How was the honeymoon?" their friends at the senior center asked when they returned home.

"Great, but we spent the first day and a half just trying to get out of the car!" replied the elderly man.

Several little girls were playing dress up. One of them put on a bridal gown and a veil. She went to show her mother how pretty she looked and said, "Look, Mommy, I'm getting marinated!"

At his wedding reception, the groom was impressed and encouraged by the way one of his elderly relatives kept referring to his wife with a multitude of endearing pet names: The love of my life, my sunshine, my princess, my sweetheart, and so on. The couple had been married almost sixty-five years.

"It's so inspiring to me that, after all of these years, you refer to your wife with such special nicknames!" said the groom. "You are obviously still very much in love!"

"To tell you the truth," the old man said dismally, "I forgot her name about fifteen years ago!"

After the ceremony, the bride turned to her new husband and asked if he would still love her even when her hair turned gray.

"I don't see why not," the groom replied. "I've loved you through four different colors already!"

A couple sat down to eat their first meal as newlyweds. The wife said, "Today I learned how to make meat loaf and chocolate cake."

The husband looked at his plate and said, "That's great, honey! Which one is this?"

At a wedding, a distant relative of the bride was sitting at a table with a bunch of family members. The bride and groom were making their rounds to greet each guest. When they got to his table they overheard him saying it was soon to be his fiftieth anniversary.

"Wow, what an inspiration!" said the bride. "Will you be doing anything special?"

"Well, I took my wife to New York City for our fortieth anniversary," the man said. "So maybe I'll go pick her back up and bring her home for our fiftieth!"

Before the wedding, a man yearns for the woman that he loves. After the wedding, the *y* becomes silent.

Marriage is an institution in which a husband loses his bachelor's degree and the wife gets her master's.

The bride was horrified to find this typo on her invitations:

MR. AND MRS. COLLINS REQUEST YOUR *PRESENTS* AT THE WEDDING OF THEIR DAUGHTER.

Another wedding invitation gone bad! This error would never be forgotten:

PLEASE JOIN US FOR THE WEDDING OF CALEB CARTER, THE *SIN* OF MR. AND MRS. FRANK CARTER.

"Let us join the happy couple in the celebration of their wedding and bring their happiness to a conclusion!" announced a preacher whose face turned beet-red after he realized what he had said.

After the wedding vows were finished, a tongue-tied preacher announced this to the congregation:

"Please remain seated until the end of the recession."

"Mommy?" asked a little girl attending her first wedding. "If he is really the best man, why isn't the bride marrying him instead?"

Two young sisters were "playing wedding" with a few neighbor boys from down the street. One was the groom and the other was the best man. After the play ceremony, they went to eat their lunch. One little boy, still in "best man" character, held up his sandwich and said in all seriousness, "I would like to propose to some toast."

A young couple went to the county clerk's office to get their marriage license. After recording all of the information, the clerk handed them the marriage license and said, "No refunds, exchanges, or warranties."

"Marriage is a union of heart, soul, and minds," said the preacher during a wedding.

An old man sitting in the audience leaned over and whispered to the guy beside him, "But just wait till they have to start paying those union dues!"

✛ ✛ ✛

A young man couldn't decide which girl to marry. He liked one girl, but he really liked another one named Maria, too. He decided to ask his friend for advice. "How do you make important decisions?" he asked his friend.

"Well, I go to church," replied his friend. "Then I look up and pray and usually the answer just comes to me."

The young man decided to try just that. He went to church, looked up to pray, and the answer was written in gold above a stained-glass window.

It said: AVE MARIA.

Funerals

"ONE THING IS FOR SURE. . .WE WILL SORELY MISS. . .
AAH, ER, UH. . .OLD WHAT'S-HIS-NAME."

Two wicked brothers who were very wealthy used their money to cover up their evil ways. They went to the same church and appeared to be perfect Christian gentlemen. The elderly pastor of their church was not aware of their wickedness. When the time came for the pastor to retire, a new pastor was hired who turned out to be very wise and intuitive. He saw right through the two brothers and didn't mind telling them so. The new pastor was a great preacher and the church outgrew its old building. A campaign was started to raise funds for a new building. Suddenly, one of the brothers died of a heart attack. The day before the funeral, the other brother went to the pastor and handed him a check for the entire amount needed to complete the building project. The pastor was stunned.

"I only have one condition," the evil brother said. "You must tell everyone that my brother was a saint during the funeral."

The pastor nodded and slipped the check in his pocket.

At the funeral the next day, the pastor gave a full salvation message. Then he spoke about the deceased wicked man.

"He was an evil man," the pastor said. "He used his money as a cover for his wickedness. He cheated and lied and swindled. But compared to his brother. . .he was a saint!"

Immediately following the graveside service, there was a huge burst of thunder followed by a lightning bolt and more thunder. The widowed husband looked at the pastor and matter-of-factly said, "Well, she's there."

A mother was driving with her young son to a funeral for a distant relative. Since the five-year-old boy had never been to a funeral, the mother took the time to explain what happened at the service and what happens to people when they die. At the grave site, the mother realized that her explanation hadn't been as thorough as she thought when her son leaned over and, in a voice loud enough for all to hear, asked, "Mom? What's in the box?"

Two elderly men were walking away from their best friend's funeral.

"Well, I wonder who will be next. I'm gettin' up there and you're way past over the hill," one old man said.

"It's better to be over the hill than under it!" his friend replied.

An elderly man, knowing he was at the end of his life, was in bed at his home just waiting for death to claim him. His wife was in the kitchen baking cookies. He could smell the delicious aroma of his favorite cookies and decided that he wanted one last cookie before he died. His wife was unable to hear his quiet raspy voice as he called out for a cookie, so he mustered up enough strength to climb into his wheelchair and wheel out into the kitchen. He lifted his thin arm to the cookie sheet and grabbed hold of a large, warm, chocolate-chip cookie. Just then his wife gently whacked his hand with her spatula.

"What was that for?" he gasped.

"Those are for the funeral," she replied.

"Son, do you believe in life after death?" the boss asked his youngest employee.

"Yes, sir," the boy replied.

"Well, good!" said the boss with a scowl. "Because just after you left early yesterday to go to your grandmother's funeral, she stopped in to see you!"

An old businessman, near death, called for his brother to come to his side.

"Please see that I'm cremated," he told his brother.

"What should I do with your ashes?" his brother asked.

"I would like you to put them in an envelope and send them to the IRS with a note that says: 'Here. Now you have everything.' "

A middle-aged man went to the doctor for his annual checkup. His wife went along. After the man's physical, the doctor called the wife into his office alone.

"Your husband seems to have a very high anxiety level and it isn't good for his heart," the doctor told her. "If you don't do the following, your husband will surely die." The doctor then handed her this list:

1. Every morning, fix him a fresh, healthy breakfast.
2. Be kind to him all day and do everything to keep his stress level to a minimum.
3. For lunch, make him a nutritious meal.
4. For dinner, prepare him whatever meal he might desire.
5. Keep the house as peaceful as possible and allow him to rest as much as he wants.
6. Don't allow him to do any chores or anything that might cause undue stress.

On their way out of the doctor's office, the husband asked his wife what the doctor said to her.

"I'm afraid you're going to die," she replied.

A young entrepreneur was alarmed at the card he received at the opening of his new store. Along with some beautiful flowers, there was a card that read: "In Deep Sympathy."

Just then, the telephone rang. It was the florist wanting to apologize for sending the wrong card.

"No problem at all," said the entrepreneur. "These things happen."

"I accidentally sent your card to a funeral," the florist explained.

"Well, what did it say?" asked the entrepreneur.

" 'Congratulations on your new location,' " came the florist's reply.

✛ ✛ ✛

A new pastor was asked to perform a funeral for a man that he had never met before. Unable to say anything about the man himself, he asked those present to share.

"Is there anyone here who can say something good about this man?" the pastor asked. There was no response.

"Well, is there someone here who can say something halfway decent about this man?" the pastor asked again. There was nothing but silence from the crowd.

"Is there anyone here who can say anything at all that is at least somewhat positive about this man?" the pastor implored.

Finally, an older gentleman stood up and said, "Well, he wasn't quite as bad as his father!"

A stingy old businessman had a terminal illness. He decided that he would disprove the statement "You can't take it with you." He had his wife go to the bank and withdraw as much money as she could fit in a pillowcase. He told her to place the money in the attic directly above his bed. His plan was to reach out and grab it on his way up to heaven when he died. A few months after the funeral, the man's wife was cleaning out the attic. Having forgotten all about her husband's silly request, she spotted the pillowcase stuffed with bills.

"I had a feeling I should have put the money in the basement," she muttered.

An old Christian cowboy once told his great-grandson his secret to living a long life: "Sprinkle a pinch of gun powder on your cereal every morning."

One hundred years later, the grandson finally died, having taken his great-grandfather's advice. He left behind ten children, thirty-five grandchildren, sixty great-grandchildren, thirteen great-great-grandchildren, and an eighty-foot hole where the crematory used to be.

There was a man who had to go to his relative's graveside service at seven o'clock in the morning. He was not happy about it at all. He wasn't a "mourning" person.

At the funeral for a middle-aged farmer, the new country preacher talked at length of the good traits of the departed. The preacher told of what a hard worker and an honest man he was. He also said the farmer was a loving husband and a kind father.

The farmer's widow could take it no more. She leaned over and whispered to one of her sons, "Will you go up there and look in that casket? See if that's your pa."

An attorney attended the funeral of a rich client. A partner of the attorney's arrived late and took a seat beside him in the back of the church. He turned to his partner and whispered, "What have I missed?"

The lawyer nodded toward the preacher and whispered back, "He just opened for the defense."

Two elderly sisters were driving in the procession to the cemetery after a distant relative's funeral. One sister realized that she had forgotten to take her medication. Not having a choice in the matter, the women turned around and headed for home, which was at least forty-five minutes away. The women had driven for about ten minutes when the sister who was driving looked in her rearview mirror. The rest of the procession was still following her.

Three men were traveling to the lake for a fishing trip. Many topics of discussion came up as they drove along. They began talking about their funerals and what they would like people to say about them when they were gone.

The first guy said, "I would like to hear them say that I was a great doctor, and a good husband and father."

The second guy said, "I would like to hear that I was a wonderful teacher who inspired kids to do great things."

The last guy replied, "I would like to hear them say, 'Look! He's still breathing!' "

After a relative's funeral, an old businessman took his young grandson for a walk around the cemetery. The man was pointing out various friends and relatives that had passed on. Pausing before one gravestone, he said, "There lies an honest man. He died owing me $10,000, but he struggled to the very end to pay off his debts. He was a good man and if anyone has gone to heaven, he has."

They kept walking and came to another gravestone.

The man said, "This man was not a very honest man at all. He owed me $15,000 and he died having done

"SISTER ALICE KEPT TELLING US HER FEET WERE KILLING HER. WE SHOULD HAVE LISTENED."

everything he could to get out of his debt. If anyone has gone down below, he has."

"Well, Grandpa," said the young boy. "You are very lucky then."

"Why's that?" asked the old man.

"Whichever place you end up in, you'll have some money to draw on!" replied the boy.

"And how are you, my dear?" a kind relative asked a widowed woman at her husband's funeral.

"Good as can be expected, I guess," replied the old woman. "I'll miss him dearly, but it was his time to go."

"Are you in pretty good health?" the relative asked.

"Well, my eyes are so bad I can hardly tell what I'm eating. My hands shake so much that I can't drink anything hot. My medicine makes me dizzy and I can't turn my neck because of my arthritis. But thank the good Lord, I can still drive!"

A man told his two brothers that he wanted to be buried at sea along the coast of Maine rather than in the church cemetery. The brothers both drowned trying to dig the grave.

At a funeral the pastor was trying to explain that, although the body is dead, the soul has departed and gone on into eternity.

"What you see here is just the shell," he said. "The nut has departed."

+ + +

"My father and old Mr. Adams have been arguing for twenty years," said a man to his friend. "But they finally stopped."

"Why?" asked his friend. "Did they bury the hatchet?"

"No, they buried Mr. Adams."

+ + +

The wife of a preacher passed away unexpectedly. The distraught pastor sent a note to the headquarters of his denomination that read: "I regret to inform you of the recent death of my wife. Could you please send me a substitute for this weekend?"

+ + +

Here lies Mrs. Morgan. She lived with her husband for fifty years and died confidently in the hope of a better life.

+ + +

A young boy and his friends were filling in a hole in his backyard when his neighbor happened to see them.

"What are you doing, boys?" his neighbor asked.

"We're having a funeral for my goldfish," replied the

boy with a sob. "He just died and we buried him."

"That's a really big hole for just a little goldfish!" the neighbor said looking at the large mound of dirt.

"That's because he's inside your cat!" said the boy.

On an atheist's tombstone was inscribed the following: ALL DRESSED UP AND NO PLACE TO GO. Scribbled underneath was this: "or so she thought!"

Two elderly women were headed to a good friend's funeral. They were reminiscing on the good times and discussing how the years had flown by.

"I wonder which one of us will go next?" asked one of the women.

"Could be either of us," replied her friend. "Once you're over the hill, you pick up speed!"

An inexperienced preacher was to hold a graveside burial service at a paupers' cemetery for an indigent man with no family or friends. Not knowing where the cemetery was, he made several wrong turns and got lost. When he eventually arrived an hour late, the hearse was nowhere in sight, the backhoe was next to the open hole, and the workmen were sitting under a tree eating lunch.

The diligent young pastor went to the open grave and found the vault lid already in place. Feeling that he should conduct the service despite his tardiness, he preached an impassioned and lengthy service, sending the deceased to the great beyond in style.

As he returned to his car, he overheard one of the workmen say to the other, "I've been putting in septic tanks for twenty years and I ain't never seen anything like that."

✠ ✠ ✠

Epitaph

REMEMBER MAN, AS YOU WALK BY,
AS YOU ARE NOW, SO ONCE WAS I,
AS I AM NOW, SO SHALL YOU BE,
REMEMBER THIS AND FOLLOW ME.

A thinking individual added a note to the tombstone:

"To follow you I'll not consent,
Until I know which way you went."

✠ ✠ ✠

A woman in Brooklyn decided to prepare her will and make her final requests. She told her pastor she had two final requests. First, she wanted to be cremated, and second, she wanted her ashes scattered all over her favorite department store.

The pastor found that odd and asked, "Why there?"

"So I'll be sure my daughters visit me twice a week."

✚ ✚ ✚

An elderly woman, who never married, died. She left
handwritten instructions for her memorial service, telling
her pastor to line up an all-female pallbearing team.
"They wouldn't take me out while I was alive," the
spinster had written. "I don't want them to take me out
when I'm dead!"

The End of the World

"SORRY, BUDDY, I CAN'T POSSIBLY HAVE THAT SIGN FOR YOU BEFORE NEXT WEEK."

Many years ago the northern lights were much more brilliant. One night a young man went out and saw them shining brightly. He assumed they signaled the end of time. He ran through his community admonishing the people to wake up. He arrived at the house of an old man and began pounding on the door. "Get up!" he shouted. "The day of judgment has come!"

"Go back to bed," the old man grumbled. "Who ever heard of the day of judgment coming in the middle of the night?"

A Bible study group was discussing the unforeseen possibility of sudden death. "We will all die some day," the leader of the discussion said, "and none of us really knows when, but if we did, we would all do a better job of preparing ourselves for that day." Everybody nodded their heads in agreement with this comment.

"What would you do if you knew you only had four weeks of life left before your great judgment day?" the leader asked the group.

"For those four weeks, I would go out into my community and witness to those that have not yet accepted Jesus into their lives," one person said.

"A very wise thing to do," said the group leader. And all the group members agreed that would be a very good thing to do.

"For those four weeks, I would dedicate all of my remaining time to being of more service to others," said another woman.

"That's wonderful!" the group leader commented, and all the group members agreed.

One gentleman in the back finally spoke up loudly. "For those four weeks, I would travel throughout the

United States with my mother-in-law in an economy car, and stay in a cheap motel every night."

Everyone was puzzled by his answer. "Why would you do that?" the group leader asked curiously.

"Because," the man smiled sarcastically, "it would be the longest four weeks of my life."

How the Media Would Cover the End of the World:

USA Today: We're Dead
The Wall Street Journal: World Ends; Stock Market Crashes
Microsoft Systems Journal: Apple Loses Market Share
Sports Illustrated: Game Over
Wired: The Last New Thing
Rolling Stone: The Grateful Dead Reunite
Reader's Digest: 'Bye
Discover Magazine: How Will the Extinction of All Life as We Know It Affect the Way We View the Cosmos?
TV Guide: Death and Damnation: Nielsen Ratings Soar!
Ladies' Home Journal: Lose 15 lbs. By Judgment Day with Our Improved "Armageddon" Diet!
Inc. Magazine: Ten Ways You Can Profit from the Apocalypse

Two Irishmen visited America. They had never seen a train before, but the hotel they chose was right beside a railroad. About midnight a train came roaring past. One man jumped up, ran to the window, and looked out. The firebox was open and the fire shining, and sparks were flying from the engine. This train was barely past when another came roaring through. The same man ran over and shook his friend awake.

"Wake up!" he cried. "They're moving hell, and three loads have already gone by!"

A pastor was preaching about judgment day. "Thunder will roar, flames will flash across the sky. Floods, storms, devastation such as you've never seen. . . " he continued dramatically.

Wide-eyed, a young boy turned to his mother. "Will I get to skip school that day?" he whispered.

A vicar was talking to one of his parishioners. The vicar said, "When you get to my age you spend a lot more time thinking about the hereafter."

"How do you feel about that?" inquired the parishioner.

The vicar replied, "Well, I often find myself going into a room and thinking: *What did I come in here after?*"

Plan ahead—it wasn't raining when Noah built the ark.

An old-time hellfire and brimstone preacher was

describing the events of judgment day and, of course, he used biblical phraseology whenever he could.

"Oh, my friends," he intoned, "imagine the suffering of the sinners as they find themselves cast into the outer darkness, removed from the presence of the Lord and given to eternal flames. My friends, at such a time there will be weeping, wailing, and a great gnashing of teeth!"

At this point, one of the elders of the congregation interrupted. "But Preacher," she said, "what if one of those hopeless sinners is toothless?"

The preacher banged the pulpit and roared, "My friends, the Lord is not put out by details. Rest assured. . . teeth will be provided!"

Why does the end of time seem so far away?

Because we say, "*Armageddon* there."

An older church woman went to the doctor and received plastic surgery—specifically, a "tummy tuck." She continued to have liposuction performed on her hips and thighs and then went out and bought several hundred dollars' worth of skin-care products and facial creams.

Another church member was astonished and asked her why she went to so much trouble to remain young looking. The older woman replied, "I heard the preacher say that Jesus was coming back soon and He's looking for a church without a spot or wrinkle."

A pastor and a couple deacons were standing by the side of the road, pounding a sign into the ground that read: THE END IS NEAR! TURN YOURSELF AROUND NOW—BEFORE IT'S TOO LATE!

A car raced past and the indignant driver yelled, "Leave us alone, you religious nuts!" From the curve they heard screeching tires and a big splash.

The pastor turned to a deacon and asked, "Do you think maybe we should have just written BRIDGE OUT on our sign?"

✝ ✝ ✝

Two boys were walking through the woods looking for walnuts. Along the way, they filled their buckets, shirts, pockets, and whatever else they could. When they could hold no more nuts, they started down the country road until they came to the cemetery. The boys decided this was as good a place as any to stop and rest and divide out the nuts.

The two boys sat in the shade of a large tree and dumped all of their nuts into a large pile. In the process, two of the nuts rolled away and rested near the road. The boys then proceeded to divide out the nuts. "One for you. One for me. One for you. One for me." As they were doing this, another boy was passing by and happened to hear them. He looked into the cemetery, but could not see the boys because they were obscured by the tree. He hesitated a moment and then ran back to town. "Dad, Dad!" he yelled as he entered his house. "The cemetery. Come quick!"

"What's wrong?" his father asked.

"Can't explain now," the boy frantically panted. "Let's just go!" The boy and his father ran up the country road and stopped when they reached the cemetery. They stopped at the side of the road and became quiet for a few moments. Then the father asked his son what was wrong.

"Do you hear that?" he whispered. Both listened intently until they heard the boys. "One for me. One for you. One for me. One for you. . .One for you. One for me. One for you. . ."

The boy then exclaimed, "The devil and the Lord are dividing the souls!"

The father was skeptical but silent—until a few moments later as the boys completed dividing out the nuts and one boy said to the other, "Now, as soon as we get those two nuts down by the road, we'll have them all."

Heaven

"LOOK, HAROLD, WE FINALLY MADE IT TO A GATED COMMUNITY."

After a long illness, a woman died and went to heaven. While she was waiting for Saint Peter to greet her, she peeked through the pearly gates.

When Saint Peter came by, the woman said to him, "This is such a wonderful place. How do I enter?"

"You have to spell a word," Saint Peter told her.

"Which word?" the woman asked.

"Love."

The woman correctly spelled "*l-o-v-e*," and Saint Peter gladly welcomed her into heaven.

About a year later, Saint Peter came to the woman and asked her to watch the gates of heaven for him that day.

While the woman was guarding the gates, her husband arrived. "I'm surprised to see you," the woman said. "How have you been?"

"Oh, I've been doing pretty well since you died," her husband told her. "I married the beautiful young nurse who took care of you while you were ill. And then I won the lottery. I sold the little house you and I lived in and bought a big mansion. And my wife and I traveled all around the world. While we were on vacation, I went water skiing today. I fell, the ski hit my head, and I drowned. Here I am now. What do I have to do to get in?"

"You have to spell a word," the woman told him.

"Which word?" her husband asked.

"*Czechoslovakia.*"

Working for God on earth usually doesn't pay a lot, but His retirement plan is out of this world.

"Now, how many of you want to go to heaven?" asked the Sunday school teacher. All the children raised their hands except one little girl.

"I'm sorry, I can't. My mommy told me to come right home after Sunday school."

✚✚✚

A teacher asked the children in her Sunday school class, "If I sold all I own and had a big garage sale and gave all my money to the church, would I get into heaven?"

"NO!" the children all answered.

"If I cleaned the church every day, took care of the yard, and kept everything neat and orderly, would I get into heaven?"

Again, the answer was "NO!"

"Well," she continued, "then how can I get to heaven?"

In the back of the room, a small boy shouted out, "You gotta be dead!"

✚✚✚

A man dies and goes to heaven where Peter meets him at the pearly gates. Peter says, "You need 1000 points to make it into heaven. You tell me all of the good things you've done, and I give you a certain number of points for each item. When you reach 1000 points, you get in."

"Okay," the man says, "I was happily married to the same woman for fifty years and never cheated on her, not even in my mind."

"That's wonderful," says Peter, "that's worth two

points!"

"Two points?" he says. "Well, I attended church all my life and gave my ten percent tithe faithfully."

"Terrific!" says Peter. "That's definitely worth a point."

"One point? My goodness! Well, what about this: I started a soup kitchen in my city and worked in a shelter for the homeless?"

"Fantastic, that's good for two more points," he says.

"TWO POINTS!" the man cries. "At this rate the only way I can get into heaven is by the grace of God!"

"Now that's what we're looking for! Come on in!"

A wealthy man died and went to heaven. He was met at the pearly gates by Saint Peter who led him down the streets of gold. They passed mansion after mansion until they came to the very end of the street. Saint Peter stopped the rich man in front of a little shack.
"This belongs to you," said Saint Peter.

"Why do I get this ugly thing when there are so many mansions I could live in?" the man demanded.

"We did the best we could with the money you sent us!" Saint Peter replied

An elderly woman in her nineties had a visitor from her church come to see her at the nursing home.

"How are you?" the visitor asked.

"Oh," said the elderly woman, "I'm just worried sick!"

"You look like you're in good health. They take good

care of you here, don't they?"

"Oh, yes, they take good care of me here."

"Do you have any pain?" the visitor asked.

"No, I can't say as I do," the elderly woman replied.

"Then what has you worried sick?" the visitor asked.

The elderly woman leaned in and explained. "All of my closest friends have already died and gone to heaven. I'm sure they are all wondering where I went!"

An exasperated mother, whose son was always getting into trouble, asked him, "How do you expect to get into heaven?"

The young boy thought for a minute and said, "Well, I'll just keep slamming the front door and running in and out until Saint Peter says, 'For heaven's sake, come in or stay out!'"

The pastor was just ending his children's sermon about heaven. After he prayed, he asked, "So kids, where do you want to go?"

"Heaven!" the kids yelled.

"And what do you have to be to get there?" asked the pastor.

"Dead!" shouted a little boy.

A family was having a fun day at the beach when the youngest child happened to notice a dead seagull lying in the sand. Heartbroken over the situation, the young child ran to her mommy and asked, "What could have happened to him?"

Not sure what to say, her mother hesitated and then said, "He died and went to heaven, honey."

This seemed to please the young girl for a moment but then she asked, "Did God throw him back down?"

A doctor, a nurse, and the president of a health insurance company died and were met by Saint Peter at the pearly gates.

Saint Peter asked the doctor, "What did you do on earth?"

The doctor replied, "I healed the sick and worked at a clinic so that if patients could not pay I would help them for free."

"You may enter," said Saint Peter.

Then he asked the nurse what she did on earth.

"I also helped heal the sick and volunteered my time at a free clinic," she replied.

"What did you do on earth?" Saint Peter asked the third person.

The man said, "I ran a large health insurance organization. I helped thousands of companies find cost-effective health care for their employees."

"Well, then," Saint Peter replied, "You may go in. . . but you can only stay for three days."

✝ ✝ ✝

Two eighty-year-old men had been friends since their Little League baseball days. One of them came down with a terminal illness and his best friend was with him by his deathbed.

"Will you do me a favor?" the healthy friend asked. "I'm hoping there is baseball in heaven. When you get there, can you find out and let me know somehow?"

The dying man said, "We've been friends for almost all of our lives. I will try and get your answer to you."

Several days after the old man's death, his friend was sleeping when he had a vivid dream. His lifelong friend appeared to him and said, "There is definitely baseball in heaven, my friend! The bad news is that you're pitching on Wednesday."

✛ ✛ ✛

An old couple had been married nearly sixty-five years when they were hit by a car and died. They had both been in good health due to the wife's strict diet and exercise program. They went to heaven and were in awe of the mansion that was prepared for them. They had a beautiful gourmet kitchen, an indoor swimming pool, and a master suite complete with a hot tub. The husband asked Saint Peter how much this was all going to cost.

"It's all free," Saint Peter replied. "You're in heaven now!"

They went outside to see the golf course which was directly behind their mansion. Saint Peter explained they would have golfing privileges every day and their own cart with their names on it.

"What are the greens fees?" the husband asked.

"This is heaven! You play for free, of course," Saint Peter replied.

Next they went to the clubhouse and they were just in time for the grandiose breakfast buffet complete with sausage quiche and sizzling bacon.

"How much does it cost for the buffet?" asked the husband.

"Don't you get it, dear?" his wife suddenly replied. "We're in heaven, so it must be free!"

"Well, where are all the healthy foods and low-cholesterol eggs?" the husband asked hesitantly.

"In heaven you can eat as much as you like of anything," Saint Peter replied, "and you will never gain weight or get sick. This is heaven!"

"Are you serious?" the husband said and then looked at his wife. "If it weren't for you and all your bran muffins, I could have been here twenty years ago!"

A cat died and went to heaven. Saint Peter met him at the gate and said, "You have been a good cat all of these years. Whatever you desire is yours."

"I lived all my life with a poor family on a farm," said the cat. "I had to sleep on hardwood floors, so a soft place to sleep would be wonderful." Instantly, a fluffy pillow appeared.

Several days later, a dozen mice were killed and they went to heaven. When asked by Saint Peter what they desired, they gave this answer. "All our lives we've had to run," said one mouse. "Cats, dogs, and humans were always chasing us. Could you give us some Rollerblades so we won't have to run anymore?"

Instantly, each mouse was given a set of tiny Rollerblades, one for each leg.

Several weeks later, Saint Peter decided to go and check on the cat. The cat was happily lounging on his new pillow.

"How are you doing?" asked Saint Peter. "Are you happy here?"

"Oh, I've never been happier!" said the cat. "And those Meals on Wheels you've been sending me are the greatest!"

After the birth of his baby brother, a little boy was thoroughly annoyed at all of his crying and screaming.

"Where did we get him, anyway?" he asked his mother.

"He came from heaven!" his mother replied.

"Well I can see why they threw him out!" the boy replied.

✠ ✠ ✠

Q: Does the Bible say that if you smoke you can't get in to heaven?
A: No, but the more you smoke, the faster you'll get there.

✠ ✠ ✠

Three police officers were standing in line at the pearly gates.

Saint Peter asked the first officer, "What did you do with your life?"

"I was a police officer," he responded.

"What kind of police officer?" Saint Peter asked.

"I was a vice officer. I kept drugs off the streets and out of the hands of kids."

"Welcome to heaven. You may enter the gates."

He asked the second man what he did as a police officer.

"I was a traffic officer," said the man. "I kept the roads and highways safe."

"Welcome to heaven. You may enter the gates."

He asked the third man what he did as a police officer.

"I was a military policeman, sir," replied the man.

"Wonderful! I've been waiting for you all day!" replied Saint Peter. "I need to take a break! Watch the gate, will you?"

A fellow found himself in front of the pearly gates. Saint Peter explained that it's not so easy to get into heaven. There are some criteria before entry is allowed. For example, was the man religious in life? Did he attend church? The man shook his head "No." Saint Peter told him that things weren't looking good.

Was he generous? Give money to the poor? Charities? The answer again was "No." Saint Peter wasn't very happy.

Did he do any good deeds? Help his neighbor? Anything? Again the answer was "No." Saint Peter was becoming concerned.

Exasperated, Saint Peter said, "Look, everybody does something nice sometime. Work with me, I'm trying to help. Now think!"

The man said, "There was this old lady. I came out of a store and found her surrounded by a bunch of bikers. They had taken her purse and were shoving her around, taunting and abusing her. I got so mad I threw my bags down, fought through the crowd, and got her purse back. I then helped her to her feet. I then went up to the biggest, baddest biker and told him how despicable, cowardly, and mean he was and then spat in his face."

"Wow," said Peter, "that's impressive. When did this happen?"

"Oh, about ten minutes ago," replied the man.

Two teenagers stood shivering at the pearly gates.

"What happened to you guys?" asked someone else in line.

"We went to see a movie at the drive-in," one of the teens replied.

"Which movie?" asked the guy in line.
" 'Closed for the Winter'!" replied the teen.

✛ ✛ ✛

Q: How do angels answer the phone in heaven?
A: "Halo!"

✛ ✛ ✛

A little boy learned at church that once you go to heaven, you can't return to earth. Several weeks later, his father was reclining on a new chair that massaged his back while he was sitting in it.

"I feel like I'm in heaven!" his father commented.

"You went to heaven, Daddy?" he asked in confusion. "What went wrong?"

✛ ✛ ✛

Knock, knock.
    Who's there?
    Isabelle.
    Isabelle who?
    Isabelle necessary on the pearly gates?

✛ ✛ ✛

Knock, knock.
    Who's there?
    Heaven.
    Heaven who?
    Heaven seen you for an eternity.

✛ ✛ ✛

Knock, knock.
Who's there?
Heaven.
Heaven who?
Heaven you heard how to get into heaven?

✛ ✛ ✛

Knock, knock.
Who's there?
Heaven.
Heaven who?
Heaven you heard way too many knock, knock jokes?

✛ ✛ ✛

"Is there a place up here where I can wash up?" a man asked Saint Peter before entering heaven.

"Yes, turn to your left and follow the signs that say METEOR SHOWERS," Saint Peter replied.

✛ ✛ ✛

As a boy, he had survived the terrible Johnstown, Pennsylvania, flood of 1889 and throughout his long life, he told the story to everyone he met.

When he died and went to heaven, he asked Saint Peter if he could tell everyone there the story of the big flood. Peter said it could be arranged.

"But I should warn you," Peter said, "Noah will be in the audience."

✚ ✚ ✚

A wealthy man was dying and the thought of leaving behind his money—the fruits of hard lifelong work—saddened him. So he began praying to ask if he could take his money with him to heaven.

One night, an angel appeared to the man. "I'm sorry, but the rule is that nobody brings anything to heaven with them. Your money will have to stay behind."

But the man was accustomed to getting his way in business, so he kept up his praying, increasing the urgency of his requests. After a while, the angel reappeared with a new message: "God has heard your prayers, and will let you bring one suitcase with you."

The man was thrilled, and pulled out the largest piece of luggage he had. Then he filled it with gold bars and coins. Shortly thereafter, he died.

At the gates of heaven, the man appeared with his big suitcase. Saint Peter stopped him, saying, "Wait a minute—you can't bring that in here!" But the man explained the special permission allowed by God and delivered by the angel.

"Well, okay," Peter said. "But I think I should check the contents first."

Peter laid the suitcase on its side, and popped open the lid. He stared in amazement for a moment and then exclaimed, "Pavement? You brought pavement to heaven?"

Q: Did you hear the one about heaven?
A: It's way over your head.

As a preacher began his ministry in a small church, a grouchy community member approached him.

"I hope you aren't one of them narrow-minded preachers who only thinks your church members will get to heaven."

The preacher replied, "I'm more narrow-minded than that. I doubt some of my own members will make it, either."

A cab driver at the pearly gates is invited to take a silken robe and golden staff with him into heaven. A preacher next in line is offered only a rough robe and wooden staff. Astonished, the minister argues, "But I'm a minister! You gave that cab driver a gold staff and a silk robe. Surely I rate higher than that."

Saint Peter responds matter-of-factly: "Here we are interested in results," he says. "When you preached, people slept. When that cabbie drove his taxi, people prayed."